BECOMING

A GREAT

HIGH SCHOOL

ASCD cares about Planet Earth.
This book has been printed on environmentally friendly paper.

BECOMING A GREAT HIGH SCHOOL

6 Strategies and 1 Attitude That Make a Difference

TIM R. WESTERBERG

Alexandria, Virginia USA

1703 N. Beauregard St. • Alexandria, VA 22311-1714 USA
Phone: 800-933-2723 or 703-578-9600 • Fax: 703-575-5400
Web site: www.ascd.org • E-mail: member@ascd.org
Author guidelines: www.ascd.org/write

Gene R. Carter, *Executive Director;* Nancy Modrak, *Publisher;* Scott Willis, *Director, Book Acquisitions & Development;* Julie Houtz, *Director, Book Editing & Production;* Leah Lakins, *Editor;* Reece Quiñones, *Senior Graphic Designer;* Mike Kalyan, *Production Manager;* Keith Demmons, *Typesetter*

PAPERBACK ISBN: 978-1-4166-0858-5 ASCD product #109052 n9/09
Also available as an e-book through ebrary, netLibrary, and many online booksellers (see Books in Print for the ISBNs).

Quantity discounts for the paperback edition only: 10–49 copies, 10%; 50+ copies, 15%; for 1,000 or more copies, call 800-933-2723, ext. 5634, or 703-575-5634. For desk copies: member@ascd.org.

Library of Congress Cataloging-in-Publication Data
Westerberg, Tim.
Becoming a great high school : 6 strategies and 1 attitude that make a difference / Tim R. Westerberg.
p. cm.
Includes bibliographical references and index.
ISBN 978-1-4166-0858-5 (pbk. : alk. paper) 1. School management and organization—United States. 2. Education, Secondary—United States. 3. Educational change—United States. I. Title.
LB2831.92.W47 2009
371.200973—dc22

2009018816

20 19 18 17 16 15 14 13 12 11 10 09 1 2 3 4 5 6 7 8 9 10 11 12

THIS BOOK IS DEDICATED TO MY PARENTS
WHO INSTILLED IN ME THE WORK ETHIC,
PERSEVERANCE, AND GIFT OF EDUCATION THAT
HAVE MADE POSSIBLE WHATEVER SUCCESS
I HAVE ENJOYED THUS FAR IN LIFE.

BECOMING A GREAT HIGH SCHOOL

6 Strategies and 1 Attitude That Make a Difference

ACKNOWLEDGMENTS

My thinking about the kind of high schools our students need and deserve is greatly influenced by the research, wisdom, and guidance of Robert J. Marzano. The opportunity I have had over the last several years to work with Dr. Marzano has been a gift of immeasurable proportions and one that will forever impact my work in high school reform.

In addition to Dr. Marzano, I am indebted to the other members of Marzano Research Laboratory, the ASCD What Works in Schools Cadre, and particularly Debra Pickering, for the resources, implementation strategies, presentation aids, words of advice, coaching, and friendship they have generously shared with me over the years. My gratitude goes out to Drs. Marzano and Pickering, and the other members of the Marzano Research Laboratory and WWIS Cadre teams. Their help made this book and the work that follows possible.

I would also like to acknowledge the contributions that the members of the faculty and staff at Littleton High School made to what this book has to offer. A great deal of what I know and believe about creating great high schools I learned from watching and listening to them.

FOREWORD
BY ROBERT J. MARZANO

High schools are in the spotlight, and virtually all high schools, even high schools that have longstanding reputations in their communities as "good schools," are under pressure to get better. Among the major sources of this pressure to improve—a force that few in leadership positions in a high school community can afford to ignore—are the No Child Left Behind Act, state accountability report cards, competition for students created through ever-expanding choice initiatives, and fears of losing our competitive advantage in the 21st century global economy.

While the forces of change are many, the "remedies" proposed to improve high schools are legion. What high school leaders and leadership teams wishing to significantly improve their schools need is a comprehensive and practical research-based model to guide them to those strategies and initiatives that have a proven track record of increasing student achievement. This book definitely fills that need—specifically by focusing on the 6+1 model.

Dr. Tim Westerberg, a 26-year veteran of the high school principalship and a nationally known high school reform activist, presents such a model in this book, *Becoming a Great High School*. Taken together, the research-based conclusions, recommendations, and examples in this work, briefly summarized here, provide a framework for helping any high school become a great high school.

High schools that get uncommon results from common student populations have several things in common, not the least of which is an effort-based, we-expect-success school culture. Examples from high-performing high schools—public and private; rural, suburban, and urban—of what such a culture "looks like" in practice are explored in this book. The evidence across schools is clear: Great high schools in this country engage all students in college and career-prep curricula and provide the support that students need to be successful. General and remedial tracks have no place in these schools.

In America's best high schools, curriculum, instruction, and assessment are guided by clear learning goals. However, many (if not most) high schools are activity driven. Teachers design learning activities for students based on what is usually a vague and implicit understanding on the teacher's part of what knowledge or skills are to be learned. Students are often unaware of the intended learning outcomes of these activities and adopt a check-it-off mentality toward schooling. Learning becomes secondary, at best, to checking off assignments as completed and collecting points toward a grade. By contrast, substantial increases in student achievement are being recorded by high schools that have identified a limited number of common, "big-picture" learning goals at the course, department, or building level.

With clear learning goals in place, high schools that go from good to great set out to accomplish those goals by strategically employing the instructional strategies embodied in a commonly held, research-based instructional model. There is a lot we know about how students learn, and using the science of teaching increases the chances of success in the classroom. Approaching lesson design with a common instructional model in mind not only increases student achievement directly but also has an indirect impact by providing teachers with a common language of instruction. In high schools that use professional learning communities and collaboration time productively, teacher talk focuses squarely on teaching and learning. Meaningful communication about teaching and learning—or about any other topic, for that matter—cannot happen absent the background knowledge provided by a common instructional model.

Any viable instructional model will include as components formative assessment, tracking student progress, and timely intervention. The research on providing effective feedback to students on their progress toward clearly stated learning goals suggests it may be the most powerful instructional strategy available to high school teachers. Tracking student progress at the student, classroom, and school levels has been shown to be motivating to students and provides teachers with data to inform adjustments to instruction. Teachers in high-performing high schools work in teams to design a rubric or scoring guide for each identified learning goal, develop common assessments or a bank of assessment items based on those scoring guides, administer frequent formative assessments, and track student progress based on the results of those assessments. In the best high schools in America, intervention for students who are not successful is a planned event, and arriving at course grades is part and parcel of the formative assessment process.

The final strategy in the 6+1 model invites students and teachers to celebrate success in making progress toward and accomplishing important academic and life skills learning goals. Celebrating success, done in certain ways, is rewarding, motivational, and just plain fun. It is the logical conclusion to a sequence of strategies designed to improve student learning and create the high schools of our choice.

On a personal note, I have known Tim for over two decades. This book represents a powerful combination of his considerable practical knowledge based on a highly successful 26-year career as a principal and decades of research and theory that people like me have tried to synthesize. Given that combination, this could be one of the most useful books on high school reform to date. I recommend it most highly.

1

Moving Schools from Good to Great

Why Some Companies Make the Leap . . . and Others Don't.
—*Jim Collins*

Early in this century, Jim Collins used this subtitle to challenge business leaders and those of us in the public sector, including schools, to think about what qualifies as good enough. He also encouraged business leaders to look at why some organizations rise to a high level of productivity and receive public recognition above other organizations with seemingly similar or even worse input.

Today, public pressure brought on by a host of factors, including economic competition from abroad, intensive media attention, and state and federal legislation, pushes performance expectations for schools higher than at any other time in our country's history. Maintaining an orderly environment, getting most students out of high school, helping some students get into college, and of course, winning a few ball games, is no longer good enough. Instead, all students are expected to graduate from high school, be ready to enter college or start a career, and have world-class, 21st century knowledge and skills. Failing schools are required by law to improve significantly quickly or face closure. But even schools that could afford to be somewhat complacent with the status quo because of reputations in their communities as "good schools" are feeling pressure to get better as well. In short, all schools are now being asked to rise to a level of productivity previously obtained by only a few. All schools are being asked to go from somewhere to great.

The recent surge of public pressure isn't the only reason schools are focused on improvement. Dedicated educators and leaders have always struggled with student engagement or achievement. Those educators who have made the most progress have done so with artistry and with an attitude that says, "It may not be our fault, but it is our problem." However, as important as these dedicated educators are, more than art and ownership are needed. Principals, teachers, and other school leaders need research-based guidance regarding the policies, practices, strategies, and beliefs *most likely* to produce results. Fortunately, such guidance is now available.

The last four decades of research in education have produced a treasure trove of information about how students learn, how effective schools and effective teachers work, what teachers need to do their work well, and what good leadership looks like in schools and districts. We know a lot about what works, or stated more accurately, what is *most likely* to work. Noted researcher and author Robert J. Marzano (2003) sums it up as follows:

> If we follow the guidance offered by 35 years of research, we can enter an era of unprecedented effectiveness for the public practice of education—one in which the vast majority of schools can be highly effective in promoting student learning. (p. 1)

Happily, there exists both an art and a science of teaching and learning. Notice that no guarantees are made about the science of teaching and learning, but rather only guidance on what is *most likely* to work. As Michael Fullan (2008) cautions, "the world has become too complex for any theory to have certainty" (p. 5). Robert Rubin, treasury secretary under former President Bill Clinton, said it this way:

> Once you've internalized the concept that you can't prove anything in absolute terms, life becomes all the more about odds, chances, and trade-offs. In a world without provable truths, the only way to refine the probabilities that remain is through greater knowledge and understanding. (Quoted in Fullan, 2008, p. 6)

The two greatest failures of leaders, according to Michael Fullan (2008), are "indecisiveness in times of urgent need for action and dead certainty that they are right in times of complexity" (p. 6). Fullan also cautions leaders about falling prey to delusions from ex post facto explorations of companies or leaders who are already successful. He calls this the halo effect. Here is an example of the problem: While it may be true that all high-performing schools in a given study possess a common characteristic (e.g., an intensive professional development program), it might also be true that many low-performing schools share this same characteristic. Making inferences about specific traits based on general impressions after the fact can be misleading.

The proper response to the halo effect is caution. Fullan is not suggesting that we have nothing to learn from successful organizations, in our case successful schools, but rather that we enter into such explorations with an attitude of something less than certainty. Fullan endorses the following three-step test by Pfeffer and Sutton:

> 1. Is the success you observe brought about by the practice you seek to emulate?
> 2. Why is a particular practice linked to performance improvement?
> 3. What are the downsides and disadvantages of the practice, even if it is a good one? (quoted in Fullan, 2008, p. 16)

Instead of certainty, Fullan suggests we give wisdom a try. They encourage educators to have "the ability to act with knowledge, while doubting what you know" (quoted in Fullan, 2008, p. viii). For consumers of research, Fullan reminds us to be cautious and use sound advice. When evaluating established research, teachers, building administrators, and other high school change agents are advised to ask questions, perhaps even play the role of the skeptic, before concluding that a school improvement initiative will produce the same results in their schools.

The Purpose of This Book

This book is for principals, teachers, and other members of high school leadership teams interested in using research-based strategies to take their schools from struggling, average, or even good to great. It is written for those educators who are interested in thinking as educational entrepreneurs and questioning fundamental assumptions about what is possible. It is also written with a very specific theory of action in mind—significant school improvement depends first, last, and foremost on improving the quality of instruction in classrooms. The centrality of improving instruction to any effective school improvement initiative is well documented in the science of teaching and learning. An educator's perspective on these issues is important because there are different lenses through which the research on highly effective schools can be viewed.

For example, when viewed at the 30,000 foot level, the research directs one to megastrategies such as a clear mission, a safe environment, a close student-adult relationship, the personalization of instruction, and the flexible use of resources. Although the links between these megastrategies and the strategies outlined in this book are obvious in most cases, the theory of action employed here zooms in on the classroom and the interaction between the teacher, the learner, and the curriculum.

Given that perspective, the framework for discussion in this book, the 6+1 Model for High School Reform (see Figure 1.1), consists of six instructional strategies and one attitude characteristic of high-achieving schools. Together these elements constitute a framework for success.

Figure 1.1
The 6+1 Model for High School Reform

One Attitude and Six Strategies for Moving Schools from Good to Great

One Attitude:
We Expect Success!
Six Strategies:
Strategy 1: **Developing Clear Instructional Goals**
Strategy 2: **Developing a Common Vision of Effective Instruction**
Strategy 3: **Using Frequent Formative Assessment**
Strategy 4: **Tracking of Student Progress**
Strategy 5: **Providing Timely Intervention for Struggling Students**
Strategy 6: **Celebrating Student Success**

Two truisms close out this introduction, the first from education researcher and author Michael Fullan, and the second, although well known, of less certain origins.

> The organization we currently have is perfectly designed to deliver the results we currently get. (Fullan, 2007)

> Insanity is continuing to do the same thing over and over and expecting different results. (author unknown)

Taken together, these two blinding flashes of the obvious open our minds and set the stage for taking our high schools from good or from somewhere to great.

2

Cultivating a We-Expect-Success Attitude

Robert Marzano (2003), in his meta-analysis of research on motivation, identifies five lines of research that explain our motivation to learn. One of these is attribution theory, which focuses on what students perceive to be the cause of their success or failure, such as ability, effort, luck, task difficulty, and so on. Of these, Marzano (2003) concludes

> Effort is the most useful because a strong belief in effort as a cause of success can translate into a willingness to engage in complex texts and persist over time. (p. 146)

We all know children and adults who attribute their failures and their successes to something or someone outside themselves. We have all heard people say things like, "The teacher doesn't like me," "She told us to study the wrong things," "No one in our family is good at math," "I got lucky," "The boss has it in for me because I'm a woman," or "The dog ate my homework!"

Discrimination is real in our society, and it may in fact be true that your child's teacher doesn't like him. But, individuals who overcome these barriers and succeed generally attribute their success or failure to their effort. We will hear successful people take ownership of their success by saying things like, "I didn't study enough for that test," or "I busted my behind and got that promotion I wanted!"

In the early 1980s, Carol Dweck, a Stanford psychologist, concluded that students are more motivated to achieve when they believe that intelligence is malleable rather than fixed at birth and that with hard work, they can improve their grades. Building on the research of Dweck and others, Joshua Aronson at

New York University recently conducted an experiment with 7th grade girls to determine the effects of different attribute messages on closing the gender gap in math. One group was told that intelligence is not fixed but can grow with hard work. A second group was told that their struggles at the start of middle school were to be expected, and a third group received a mix of the two messages. The fourth group, the control group, received an antidrug message. Girls in all three of the experimental groups scored significantly higher than those in the control group (Viadero, 2007, October 24).

The National Mathematics Advisory Panel weighed in on the importance of an effort-based belief system in the 2008 report *Foundations for Success*. The report states

> Children's goals and beliefs about learning are related to their mathematics performance. Experimental studies have demonstrated that changing children's beliefs from a focus on ability to a focus on effort increases their engagement in mathematics learning, which in turn improves mathematics outcomes: When children believe that their efforts to learn make them "smarter," they show greater persistence in mathematics learning. Research shows that the engagement and sense of efficacy of African-American and Hispanic students in mathematical learning contexts tend to be lower than that of white and Asian students, but also that it can be significantly increased. (p. xx)

Delivering Critical Messages

Jonathan Saphier is another of the many researchers and theorists who writes about the role of beliefs and effort-based ability. He concluded that a student's belief in his or her efforts rather than his or her innate ability is the most important determinant of student learning. He also stated that these beliefs can enable all students to do rigorous academic work at high standards. According to Saphier, in schools that embody effort-based ability

> All students receive three critical messages at every turn from every adult and from the policies, practices, and procedures of the organization:
>
> 1. What we're doing here is important.
> 2. You can do it.
> 3. I'm not going to give up on you—even if you give up on yourself. (DuFour, Eaker, & DuFour, 2005 pp. 89–90)

Educators that exhibit what Saphier (DuFour, Eaker, & Dufour, 2005) calls effort-based learning know how to effectively show their students how to

1. Say it
2. Model it
3. Organize for it
4. Protect it
5. Reward it (pp. 105–109)

For example, what message is a teacher sending to students if he communicates to the class, either explicitly or implicitly, that he expects final grades to follow the bell curve? Many students will interpret this message as, "Only a few of you can expect to get *A*s in this class." This is hardly a we-expect-success message.

Contrast that example to the message students receive when a teacher announces that he expects grades for a particular learning goal to cluster at the lower end of the scale at the beginning of instruction, approach normal distribution as different students master content and skills at different times, and follow the pattern of the J curve, with most students earning high scores by the time summative grades are posted.

Grading is but one, albeit an important, manifestation of a we-expect-success attitude. Are teachers modeling behaviors that demonstrate "What we're doing here is important" when they come to class late or unprepared, schedule a movie day, or allow students to pack up early following a test or taxing learning experience? Are teachers and administrators modeling a you-can-do-it attitude if the school's homework policy allows students to take a zero for incomplete work? Is the school organized for effort-based learning if there are policies in place that put a cap on how many students can be in college-prep or career-prep courses or policies and practices that allow for tracking and ability grouping? Are students receiving messages that say "What we're doing here is important" if classes are not protected from routine public address announcements or if early dismissal for athletic contests is a frequent occurrence? Do awards and recognition ceremonies focus only on achievement or on growth as well? All effort-based instruction should include opportunities for educators to say it, model it, organize for it, protect it, and reward it.

Promoting an Attitude of High Expectations

Testimonies that support the importance of a we-expect-success attitude are not difficult to find in the professional literature. In the High Schools for Equity study, which is an ongoing study of five urban high schools in California that have beaten the odds in helping low-income students of color succeed, Linda Darling-Hammond and Diane Friedlaender (2008) report that all five schools have three design features in common, one of which is personalization. These schools deploy a number of specific strategies to personalize education (e.g., advisories, smaller class sizes, connections with families), but the common thread that runs through all of these strategies is the expectation of success. A parent in one of the study schools expressed it this way:

> It's expected of him to perform. It's not, 'We'll see if you can do it,' but, 'You can do it and you're going to do it.' So he thinks like that now. (p. 17)

This is a great example of a we-expect-success attitude in action.

In a report from the National Association of Secondary School Principals, Jim Rourke (2007) concludes

> Successful high schools are much more than a list of strategies or activities. At their core, each of the Breakthrough High Schools demonstrates a belief that every student in the school can be academically successful. This translates into positive teacher-student relationships, which leads to a challenging learning environment in which students feel valued. Teachers work collaboratively and are passionate about preparing their students for life in the 21st century. (p. 25)

In a study reporting the likelihood of students in the Chicago Public Schools applying, being accepted, and enrolling in college, Roderick and colleagues (2008) report

> Across all our analyses, the single most consistent predictor of whether students took steps toward college enrollment was whether their teachers reported that their high school had a strong college climate, that is, they and their colleagues pushed students to go to college, worked to ensure that all students would be prepared, and were involved in supporting students in completing their college applications. (p. 4)

The study showed that the effects of a climate of high expectations were particularly pronounced for Latino students.

Jobs for the Future analyzed small schools that have been successful in closing the achievement gap in math achievement, and the results also supported effort-based learning (Goldberg, 2008). The analysis states

> A critical difference in these schools is their culture. It is their explicit mission to eliminate the psychological barriers to learning which too often are ignored in traditional schools. The staff strives to create a nurturing yet challenging atmosphere that celebrates small successes and convinces students over time that they can master a college-prep curriculum. Everyone is held to the same high standards, regardless of their entering skill levels, and regular help is available to those who need it. The belief that every student can attend college and succeed there permeates every aspect of school life. Effort, perseverance, and academic risk taking are revered. (p. 2)

The High Performing High Poverty Readiness model (HPHP) presented by Mass Insight Education and Research Institute in its 2007 report, *The Turnaround Challenge,* is constructed around nine strategies found in analyses of HPHP school practice and effective schools research (Calkins, Guenther, Belfiore, & Lash, 2007). Strategy 4, shared responsibility for achievement, is defined as "staff [members] feel deep accountability and a missionary zeal for student achievement." In a further description of this HPHP strategy, the report goes on to make the following claim:

> Virtually every 'school that works' report we reviewed for this project began its discussion of essential reform elements with the importance of 'establishing a culture of high expectations.' (p. 34)

Perri Applegate, a researcher at the University of Oklahoma K20 Center, found in a recent study of rural schools in Oklahoma that a key distinguishing factor between high-achieving and low-achieving schools was the school communities' commitment to student excellence. Applegate also reported that key stakeholders in high-achieving schools did not accept the idea that students were destined to fail based on their address. The title of Applegate's article that included the findings captures the essence of the point being made here—"Attitude determines student success in rural schools" (University of Oklahoma, 2008).

Promoting Open Enrollment in Honors, Advanced Placement, and International Baccalaureate Programs

The issues surrounding enrollment policies and practices for college-prep, career and technology, and remedial courses merit a more detailed analysis.

Research on effective schools strongly suggests that schools with a we-expect- success attitude at the heart of their cultures have policies and practices in place that encourage open enrollment in honors, Advanced Placement (AP), International Baccalaureate (IB), and 21st century career and technology (C & T) programs. A 2007 report prepared by WestEd and commissioned by the Bill and Melinda Gates Foundation analyzed common features of five high-performing high schools serving low-income and minority students and concluded that each of the schools gives students a rigorous college-preparatory curriculum (Ash, 2007, September 26). A second report by WestEd that focused on achievement in mathematics also supports the argument for a rigorous curriculum for all (Huebner & Corbett, 2008). The report states

> The math coursework a school or district offers is by far the most concrete piece of evidence of its academic plans or aspirations for its students. A recent U.S. Department of Education study found that access to academically challenging coursework in high school significantly increases the likelihood of a student successfully completing a bachelor's degree. According to the report, access to and enrollment in challenging courses had a greater impact than any other factor, including income level and parents' level of education. (p. 2)

Similar findings came out of a recent study of nine Leading Edge schools by Education Resource Strategies (Shields & Hawley-Miles, 2008) and an analysis of Breakthrough schools by the National Association of Secondary School Principals (Boone, Hartzman, Mero, & Rourke, 2008).

Researchers at the University of Texas have documented the benefits of student participation in AP programs, even for students who don't do well on the AP tests (Klein, 2007). According to their analysis, students who took at least one AP course and test had higher college GPAs and graduation rates than students who took at least one AP course but no tests. These students also had higher GPAs and graduation rates than students who did neither. Jean C. Robinson, a professor of political science at Indiana University Bloomington, addressed the fact that overall participation in the 2007 AP program was up but scores were down. She said, "Even if they don't score [well on the AP exam], they will be more successful in college than those who haven't taken the AP exam at all" (Cech, 2008, February 20). Reacting to the same data from the 2007 AP results, a superintendent from North Carolina responded, "I'd rather a student take an AP test and score a 2 than take a quote 'honors course' and get an *A* in it. That student is going to be better prepared in college." (p. 13)

Freelance writer David Whitman (2008) has identified 10 habits of highly effective urban schools based on his analysis of data captured in his visits to six high-performing urban secondary schools. They are as follows:

1. Tell students exactly how to behave and tolerate no disorder.
2. Require a rigorous, college-prep curriculum.
3. Assess students regularly, and use the results to target struggling students and improve instruction.
4. Build a collective culture of achievement and college going.
5. Reject the culture of the streets.
6. Extend the school day or year.
7. Welcome accountability for teachers and principals and embrace constant reassessments.
8. Use unconventional channels to recruit committed teachers.
9. Don't demand too much from parents.
10. Don't waste resources on fancy facilities or technology.

Some of Whitman's habits are beyond the scope of this book, and readers may disagree with his advocacy for the development of what he calls paternalistic institutions. For example, educators who subscribe to a child-centered, developmental philosophy of education might not embrace Whitman's suggestion that students should be told "exactly how to behave," and critics of zero-tolerance policies would be rebuffed by his recommendation that school officials "tolerate no disorder." But, again, a call for a we-expect-success attitude and high academic standards for all students comes through loud and clear in Whitman's list.

At Bell Multicultural School in Washington, D.C., which includes a student body with a high proportion of low-income English language learners, all students took the AP English Literature test as juniors in 2007 and were scheduled to take the AP English Language and Composition test in 2008. Even though only three students earned a passing grade on the 2007 exam, administrators at the school believe the AP courses teach more reading and writing than remedial English classes (Mathews, 2008). The vision for the Columbus Alternative High School in Ohio, which includes a student population that is 66 percent minority and 57 percent low-income, includes a structure that allows all students to be enrolled in AP courses, IB courses, or both. At Wheaton High School in Maryland, which includes a student population that is 77 percent minority and 48 percent low-income, each of the school's five academy programs requires all students to enroll in college-level instruction (e.g., honors, AP, college-level) in some form (Boone et al., 2008). Increasing opportunities for students to participate in rigorous coursework is not just an urban schools issue. Only 52 percent of rural high schools offer AP courses, placing them behind both suburban and urban schools in that regard (Dalton & Mills, 2008). Principals and teachers in schools that encourage students to go for the gold are willing to trade higher participation rates for lower average scores.

Student participation in AP and IB programs can be dramatically increased when and where the political will to do so exists. Advanced Placement Strategies Inc. worked with 10 high schools in the Dallas area and successfully increased the AP participation rates in those schools from 2,500 students in 2000 to 4,000 students in 2006, with the number of passing scores among all student groups increasing as well (Cavanagh, 2007, October 17). Teacher training, curricular support, and cash bonuses for participating students and teachers are also credited for the results.

An article in the *Washington Post* revealed that some schools in the Washington, D.C., area are abandoning honors courses as school officials push more students into AP and IB courses (de Vise, 2008). One student laments the demise of honors courses in her school with the comment, "There's some students who are just honors students. They don't have the ability to push themselves into AP. They're too smart to be in regular classes" (p. B01). Right problem, wrong solution—keep the honors courses and get rid of the regular classes.

At Littleton High School in Colorado, where I served as principal for 20 years, students are encouraged to enroll in honors, pre-IB, AP, and IB classes. The only requirement for students to get into AP English is to sign up. Students fill out an application form for the IB program, but the application is to ensure that students and their parents understand the program expectations. It is extremely rare for a student to be denied admission to the program. If a student decides he or she wants to go for the gold, perhaps even at the expense of his or her GPA, why should any teacher or administrator stand in the way?

Most high schools in our town in Colorado do not share our philosophy of inclusion. Most schools set limits on the number of sections of honors, accelerated, or college-level courses they offer. Many schools also require test scores, GPAs, writing samples, or teacher recommendations to apply for limited slots in selective courses. An often understated goal of many high schools in this country is to have a high average of student scores on AP and IB exams. At Littleton High School, faculty and staff strive to prepare students to do well on those tests, but the prize is a higher percentage of students taking those exams each year.

Putting a new title on an old syllabus does little to prepare students for post secondary education and careers. In her reaction to the lower overall scores on AP exams in 2007, Jennifer Topiel of the College Board said, "We feel very strongly that students should not be placed into AP classes without better preparation," (Cech, 2008, February 20, p. 13). Also responding to the downturn in the 2007 AP scores, Daria L. Hall of Education Trust observed

> To change these patterns we need to get serious about ensuring that college-prep coursework really provides students with what they need to be successful. Just slapping a new title on the same old courses won't boost achievement—it'll only give students a false sense of promise that they will be college-ready. (p. 13)

What do students need to be successful? In a recent commentary, Paul Von Blum (2008), senior lecturer at UCLA, bemoans what is, in his experience, a trend toward memorization, factual information, and results that strays away from inquiry, critical thought, and serious liberal learning in high school AP courses. Educators and administrators can ensure that honors, AP, IB, and other college-prep courses give students what they need to be successful by establishing a guaranteed and viable curriculum and clear instructional goals. This process will be discussed in greater detail in Chapter 3.

There are other options in addition to AP and IB courses that educators can use to ensure that students are engaged with rich curricula. Dual-credit or co-enrollment programs are rapidly increasing in popularity. These programs allow students to earn college credit while in high school by taking college courses taught at the high school, enrolling part-time in a nearby college, or participating in classes that use video conferencing.

A 2002–03 U.S. Department of Education survey revealed that 71 percent of public high schools offer dual-enrollment courses to students (Rossi, 2007). Data from that same year show that half of all U.S. colleges included high school students in their ranks ("A formula for higher learning," 2007). In five years, the number of Texas public school students enrolled in at least one dual-credit course jumped 68 percent to include more than 60,000 students in 2007 (Mellon, 2008). Records from the Iowa Department of Education showed that in 2007 high school students made up 26.2 percent of community college enrollment in that state. Three community colleges in Iowa had student enrollments that included more than 40 percent high school students (Gearino, 2007). Iowa, Massachusetts, New York, New Mexico, and Pennsylvania are among the states that have recently proposed adding millions of dollars to state budgets to expand dual-enrollment programs.

Two high schools in Utah have successfully used concurrent enrollment programs to increase academic rigor, particularly among traditionally low-performing populations (Farrace, 2008). Forest Grove High School in Oregon offered dual-enrollment opportunities to 131 students who collectively earned 1,123 credits during the 2006–07 school year. The dual enrollment program is part of a comprehensive effort to increase the rigor of the curriculum at the school, an initiative which over a four-year period has produced rather dramatic increases in graduation rates and test scores (Boone et al., 2008). By using dual-credit courses as a primary delivery mechanism, one school district in Illinois has instituted a multiyear plan for all students to graduate with college credit or a vocational certificate (Swanson, 2007).

Researchers at Columbia University conducted a study on dual-enrollment programs in Florida and New York, and they found that students in those programs were more likely to graduate from high school, enroll in postsecondary education, and stay in college than their peers who did not take dual-enrollment courses. These benefits were even more pronounced for low-income students (Arenson, 2007).

High school teachers can further enhance a dual- or concurrent- enrollment class by using college and university lectures, lecture notes, assignments, and video and audio clips available free online. One such source, the MIT high school site (see http://ocw.mit.edu/OcwWeb/hs/home/index.htn), allows teachers to search by specific course titles or topics. A teacher outside of Miami uses material from the site not only to augment her lessons but also to give students a feel for what college is like (Cavanagh, 2008, February 6). The following implications, as summarized in a recent WestEd report (Corbett & Huebner, 2007), are undeniable:

> A student's access to a high-quality academically challenging high school curriculum has been found to have the biggest influence on whether he or she will earn a college degree. It is a more important variable than either race or family income and is also more important for Black and Hispanic students than for white students. (p. 13)

Advancing 21st Century Career and Technology Programs

Not everyone agrees that all high school students should follow a college-preparatory program of study. Charles Murray, co-author of the controversial 1994 book *The Bell Curve,* argues in his new book that NCLB's target of 100 percent proficiency in reading and writing by 2013–14 is "educational romanticism," and that education policy that calls for all students to take high-level academic courses is "idiotic" (Hoff, 2008). In *Real Education,* Murray asserts that only about 10 percent of high school students can understand college material and that schools should be directing many students toward vocational programs that prepare young people for the workforce. Murray's position is extreme for many of us, but it is a strong argument that can be made for offering 21st century career and technology programs as an option for high school students.

Career and technology (C&T) programs offer yet another way to get students out of the remedial and general tracks and into a curriculum with a 21st century future. Well-designed C&T courses integrate rigorous academic content into authentic work tasks that are motivating for students. In addition to gaining lifelong skills, students can earn a lot of money in C&T fields. Data from the Washington State Department of Labor and Industries show that a journeyman refrigerator and air conditioning mechanic can earn on average $55.41 per hour (Rolph, 2008). That's more than $100,000 a year. Many positions like these go unfilled as young people seem to avoid the trades. Too many students spend their high school careers in general education tracks that do not prepare them for postsecondary education or future careers. Many of these students often waste time and money in a four-year college before dropping out and settling for a lower paying job.

According to one career counselor in Oakland, California, among students who graduate in the bottom 40 percent of their classes and then go on to four-year colleges, two-thirds had not earned degrees after eight and a half years (Nemko, 2008). That's a lot of time and a lot of money. Career and technical coursework would be a better option for many of these students.

Some combination of college-prep and C&T coursework is probably the best option for most students. Gary Hoachlander, president of ConnectEd, argues convincingly that career and technical courses should not be positioned as an alternative to college preparation, but rather that students should be offered multiple pathways that bring together challenging technical and academic courses. He says multiple pathways help students answer the "Why do I need to know this" question (Hoachlander, 2008). A new law in the state of Washington will provide $100 million dollars to regional campuses to help them expand their programs and allow students to take courses in such fields as aerospace engineering, computer networking, and healthcare. Support for the legislation is centered around the belief that properly designed C&T courses can effectively teach the academic math and reading skills that students need to be successful on the Washington Assessment of Student Learning (Rolph, 2008). James R. Stone, III and his colleagues at the National Research Center for Career and Technical Education at the University of Louisville have developed an instructional model that trains teachers to incorporate math topics into units of study where math naturally occurs in career-oriented courses. A number of states and school districts are now working with the center to train teachers in the Math in Career Education model, which has been shown to increase students' math scores (Cavanagh, 2008, March 27).

Many schools across the country are getting it right. In 2007 high schools in Virginia Beach, Virginia, awarded nearly 1,400 industry certificates in fields such as turf management and outdoor power equipment, an increase of about 500 certificates in two years (Roth, 2008). Baltimore Polytechnic Institute uses a strong C&T program to attract high-achieving students from the area to its campus. For the 2007–08 school year, 1,800 students applied for 430 freshman slots. Seventy-eight percent of the student body is African American and enrollment is split evenly between males and females. During the 2007–08 school year,

100 percent of Polytechnic's junior class passed the state's high school science exam (Trotter, 2008).

Resources are available to help educators figure out how to use C&T programs to present an engaging academic curriculum to students. Stephen Dewitt's article "Blurring the lines" offers practical advice for school administrators (Dewitt, 2008), and the National High School Center's Web site (See www.betterhighschools.org/topics/#Curriculum) is an excellent source for specific ideas on curriculum content, design, and integration.

Eliminating General and Remedial Tracks

"Slowing students down does not help them catch up."
"Students who take consumer math will never have any money."

These two statements, captured at a recent high school reform conference (Christie, 2007), humorously summarize what the research says about the impact of most remedial and many general track courses. A 2007 study by the Mitchell Institute (2007) identified academic tracking as the chief barrier to college attendance. The study showed the following facts:

> Students in a General/Vocational track are less challenged in the classroom, receive less encouragement about college, and do not feel as well-prepared for life after high school. They are less likely to aspire to college or to believe that their parents expect them to attend college, and the strength of their convictions that college is attainable and affordable is significantly lower. (pp. 1–2)

Students in general tracks fare little better than those students who are stuck in remedial tracks. A 2007 ACT report, *Rigor at Risk*, concludes that three-fourths of students who take a standard core curriculum in high school are unprepared for college (Ash, 2007, June 23). According to 2004 data from the National Center for Education Statistics, 42 percent of freshmen in community colleges and 20 percent of freshmen in public four-year institutions require remedial courses in reading, writing, or math in order to handle college-level work (Wise, 2008). Additionally, employers aren't any happier with the performance of students who use general tracks to prepare for the workforce. Data from the National Association of Manufacturers indicates that 60 percent of U.S. manufacturing companies said high school graduates were poorly prepared for entry-level jobs (Wise, 2008).

The results from international comparisons highlighted the failings of remedial and general tracks as well. Results from the 2006 Program for International Student Assessment (PISA) show that poverty in the United States has a bigger impact on student achievement than most other countries in the study. Ross Wiener of Education Trust said the exam results are not surprising given research showing that many American schools tend to provide underprivileged students with less demanding curricula, poor quality teachers, and fewer educational resources than their peers in wealthier communities. "We give students less of everything that makes a difference in school" (Cavanagh, 2007, December 12).

America's Promise Alliance included a 10–point plan for reducing dropout rates as a major component of their national agenda. Two points from that plan that directly relate to this discussion are (1) establishing a rigorous college- and work-preparatory curriculum for high school graduation and (2) expanding college-level learning opportunities in high school (*The 10-Point Plan*, n.d.). The much-heralded Vanderbilt Assessment of Leadership in Education measures how well principals implement six critical components for maximizing student achievement. One of those components is ensuring "ambitious academic content is provided to all students in core academic subjects" (Olson, 2008). However you view student preparation for postsecondary education or for 21st century careers—from the state, national, or international perspective, the conclusion is the same—remedial and general tracks do not serve students well.

I spent 20 years getting rid of remedial tracks and courses at Littleton High School. When I arrived there in 1985, the school had well-established remedial courses in math, science, English, and social studies. Officially, they were known as basic skills courses. Supposedly, students who lacked basic skills would receive necessary remediation. The problem was that participating students never got fixed. Students in 9th-grade basic skills English went on to 10th- and 11th-grade basic skills English. If they were still with us as seniors, they were placed in 12th-grade basic skills English, yet many of these students could not write a coherent nonfiction essay. It's no wonder that these students never receive these basic skills when school administrators say, "Let's put all the neediest students, several of whom have behavior problems, together in one class." What is wrong with this picture?

I seized opportunities as they presented themselves to eliminate basic skills courses. First, it was the social studies department. No one wanted to teach the basic skills sections. (We must not have had a new teacher in the department that year.) So, I said, "Good, we won't." Science remedial courses were eliminated soon after that, math came next, and finally English. In my 20th year at Littleton High School, I finally convinced the English department faculty to eliminate the last section of 9th-grade basic skills English. During this evolutionary period failure rates at the school generally declined, contrary to the fears often expressed by staff members who opposed the elimination of remedial courses.

High schools all over the country are eliminating remedial and general track courses, holding *all* students accountable for meeting challenging college- and career-prep standards, and providing the support students need to meet those standards. Some of those schools include Animo Inglewood Charter High School in Los Angeles, Stanley E. Foster Construction Tech Academy in San Diego, June Jordon School for Equity in San Francisco, Leadership High School in San Francisco, New Technology High School in Sacramento, California (Darling-Hammond & Friedlaender, 2008), Columbus Alternative High School in Ohio, Forest Grove High School in Oregon, Westwood High School in Memphis, Wheaton High School in Maryland (Boone, Hartzman, Mero, & Rourke, 2008), and Morgan County High School in Georgia ("Finalists named" 2008) to name just a few.

High-achieving schools are very deliberate about practicing the six high-leverage instructional factors included in the 6+1 Model for High School Reform, beginning with the subject to which we will now turn— clear instructional goals. But the power of these factors is severely limited if they are not practiced within a culture characterized by a we-expect-success attitude.

3

Strategy 1: Developing Clear Instructional Goals

Approaching instruction with clear instructional goals, or to borrow a phrase popularized by Stephen Covey, beginning with the end in mind, not only makes intuitive sense but is well supported by research. In his 35 years of meta-analysis on research in education, Robert Marzano (2003) identifies a guaranteed and viable curriculum as one of 11 factors with a proven track record of increasing student achievement. Marzano (2003) defines a guaranteed and viable curriculum as one in which

> 1. Clear guidance is given to teachers regarding the content to be addressed in specific courses, at specific grade levels.
> 2. Individual teachers do not have the option to disregard or replace content that has been assigned to a specific course or grade level.
> 3. The content articulated in the curriculum for a given course or grade level can be adequately addressed in the time available. (pp. 25–30)

From an operational standpoint, educators and administrators can specify the content to be covered by setting clear, doable instructional goals at the classroom, school, and district level.

Rick Stiggins (2008) argues that clear academic standards or learning goals form an essential structural foundation for a balanced assessment system. According to Stiggins, learning goals best serve the information needs of all stakeholders, including students, when they are

- Centered on the truly important learnings of the field of study
- Clearly and completely integrated into learning progressions within and across all grades
- Precisely defined so that all educators can interpret them consistently
- Created within the developmental reach of the students who are to master them
- Designed to be manageable given the teacher's available resources and students' ability to learn
- Thoroughly mastered by the designated teachers (p. 6)

Instruction and assessment in high schools that move from good to great are guided by learning goals that meet these criteria.

Fighting Curriculum Anarchy

In contrast to the instructional clarity described above, Jerald Craig (2003) calls the following actions curriculum anarchy. He says

> Decisions about what to teach in each grade are left up to schools, many of which pass the choice on to teachers. The result is an uneven hodgepodge of instructional aims and subject matter, with content and expectations varying sharply from classroom to classroom and from school to school. [This is] curriculum anarchy. (p. 13)

Hodgepodge and *curriculum anarchy* are very dramatic words to use to describe what is going on in today's classrooms; however, this language accurately reflects the lack of instructional clarity evident in most high schools in this country. Consider the following examples from the well-respected suburban high school in Colorado where I served as principal for 20 years.

At Littleton High School we offered a class titled "Contemporary Political and Economic Issues," which was a one-semester, senior-level social studies course required for graduation. In other words, our social studies department convinced the board of education that the content of this class was so important to our students, so critical to the preservation of the American way of life, so essential to democracy in the free world (I can use dramatic language, too) that students could not leave school without it. Three individuals taught the course, all of whom were truly excellent teachers in every sense.

I asked them one day, "What is it about Contemporary Political and Economic Issues that is guaranteed across all three teachers? What are the six or eight big-picture outcomes that are constant for all students, regardless of which teacher the computer assigns them?" Their answer was "Nothing." They went on to explain that they had tried over the years to identify common instructional goals and performance standards but couldn't agree. They agreed that the course was very different depending on which teacher taught it. So, we told students and parents that there were things about Contemporary Political and Economic Issues that were so important students could not graduate without them, but as a staff we didn't know what they were? That's nuts! This was an example of curriculum anarchy. The teachers later recommended removing the course from the list of courses required for graduation.

A second example from Littleton's math department drives the point home. A parent called me to express her concerns about the grade her 9th-grade son had received during his first semester in Honors Advanced Algebra. He received a *B*. She said it wasn't the *B* she was complaining about (although I suspected that at some level it was) but rather the inconsistency of the school's grading practices. Her son finished the semester with a 91 percent and received a *B*. His friend, who had taken the same course but from the teacher across the hall, also had a 91 percent but received an *A*. One teacher had a policy of awarding *A*s for students who received 92 percent and above, while the other teacher gave *A*s to students who achieved 90 percent and above.

The parent said, "That's not fair." I agreed. The parent responded, "You ought to have a common grading scale at that school so that a student who receives 91 percent earns the same grade from all teachers. I don't care if it's an *A* or a *B*, but it ought to be the same." I said "No." "No?" she questioned.

Every teacher, counselor, administrator, and most students, know that a 91 isn't a 91 just because of a common schoolwide grading policy. I can make a 91 percent so difficult that no one gets an *A* or so easy that everyone gets one. Any semblance of consistency and fairness in grading comes about only when teachers are meeting at least twice a month to identify clear course- or grade-level instructional goals and clear standards or criteria for what success looks like.

A common grading scale, based in some form on the traditional 100-point scale, is subjectivity masquerading as objectivity. It may fool parents, but those inside the schools know better.

I rejected the parent's proposed solution of a common grading scale because it would have let us off the hook by hiding the problem. Instead, I told her that those two teachers would begin working to address the aforementioned issues within the next week. First, they would begin the discussion with just the two of them, and then with the other members of the mathematics department. I told her that I would be monitoring their progress. Did that process guarantee that outcomes and standards would be exactly the same across all teachers of the same course? No, but it got us a lot closer to that goal than our adopting a schoolwide grading system would have.

Corbett and Huebner (2007) provide the following definition for curriculum coherence based on their study of high-achieving high schools. They say

> Coherence means that courses follow one another in a logical sequence. It means school teams have discussed and agreed what content should be covered in each course, how it generally should be taught, and how well students should be expected to learn it. (p. 20)

Will your school have curriculum coherence or curriculum anarchy? This is the first decision that any school wanting to become a great school has to make.

Challenging a Been There, Done That Attitude

When we begin discussing the merits of a guaranteed curriculum, many educators and administrators will react with one or more of three dismissive responses.

The first response is a been-there, done-that response. I will hear many teachers or administrators say things like, "The district made us do that curriculum mapping stuff (or some similar activity) two years ago." In today's standard-based world you have probably been there, but have you really done that? Here is the distinction.

Doug Reeves (2008) uses his research on the degree of implementation of school reform efforts to highlight what he calls "the myth of linearity." This belief, one that Reeves argues is accepted by most would-be education reformers, is that greater implementation leads to greater student achievement in a linear fashion. That is, if we implement a particular research-based reform a little, we will see a little improvement in student achievement. If we implement the reform to a moderate degree, we can expect a moderate increase in student achievement, and if we invest in extensive implementation, we will be rewarded with a substantial increase in achievement.

Unfortunately, this is a myth. Instead, Reeves's research shows that the relationship between degree of implementation and student achievement is nonlinear. In other words, we shouldn't expect to see any change in student achievement until we get to extensive implementation. The good news, Reeves says, is that something akin to a guaranteed and viable curriculum (i.e., instructional goals, performance standards, aligned curricula, and assessments) exists in almost every school district. The bad news is that the degree of implementation in the vast majority of cases is far short of extensive (i.e., some teachers implement some items in some departments or new teachers use a certain technique but veteran teachers do not). Curricular implementation that is not extensive produces flat student achievement trends and creates reform fatigue among teachers and administrators. Deep implementation of a few things in the curriculum beats superficial implementation of many things. A guaranteed and viable curriculum—you've been there, but have you done that *extensively*?

Moving Beyond Using State Standards as the Guaranteed and Viable Curriculum

The second dismissive response that inevitably crops up in any discussion on focusing instruction and assessment squarely on a set of collaboratively developed instructional goals is, "We have state standards, so we don't have to create our own guaranteed and viable curriculum." Opponents will also say, "The state has already given us one, thank you very much." State standards alone do not constitute a guaranteed and viable curriculum. State standards documents typically include

1. Too many standards
2. Standards that are not of equal importance
3. Standards that lack unidimensionality
4. Standards that allow for vastly different expectations for students that vary between teachers

Too Many Standards Are Included

In many states, there are simply too many standards to serve as a viable curriculum. If the curriculum isn't viable, individual teachers have to decide what to leave out, and guaranteed standards go out the window. Researchers at Mid-continent Research for Education and Learning (McREL) examined national and state standards documents and identified 200 standards and 3,093 benchmarks in 14 subject areas. They estimated that to teach all those standards and benchmarks would require 71 percent more instructional time than is currently available, which would necessitate the equivalent of a K–21 or K–22 school system (Marzano & Haystead, 2008). Although a few parents might approve, we would no doubt be hard pressed to convince taxpayers and students to forestall high school graduation until age 28.

Cynthia Schmeiser, president and chief operating officer of ACT's education division, commented on the problem of state curricula that include too many standards. She said

> State learning standards are often too wide and not deep enough. [High school teachers] are trying to cover too much ground—more ground than colleges deem necessary—in the limited time they have with students. (Olson, 2007, p. 20)

Few teachers would argue with Schmeiser. Too many standards spoil the schools.

All Standards Are Not Equally Important

I asked thousands of teachers and other educators in workshops I have conducted the following question: "Are all of your state standards of equal importance, as measured either by their usefulness to students after high school or by the emphasis they receive on your state assessment?" I have yet to receive my first affirmative response.

During a presentation to middle and high school teachers and administrators in Breckinridge, Colorado, Willard Daggett (2007) asked conference participants which of the following sets of outcomes are most important to graduates after high school:

1. Knowledge in one discipline
2. Application within one discipline

3. Application across disciplines
4. Application to real-world predictable situations
5. Application to real-world unpredictable situations

Of course, everyone chose the outcomes for answers 4 and 5.

Next, he asked, "Which of the sets of outcomes are emphasized most on your state tests?" Predictably, nearly everyone in attendance picked the set containing outcomes 1 and 2. State standards and tests, Daggett says, are the beginning, not the end of a coherent curriculum.

ACT's 2005–06 National Curriculum study showed that college instructors largely disapproved of their state's academic content standards. Two-thirds of those who responded said their state standards prepared students "poorly" or "very poorly" for college-level work. High school teachers, on the other hand, felt differently, with a majority responding that their state standards prepared students "well" or "very well" for college-level work (Marklein, 2007). Not all state standards are of equal importance, and what students get tested on may not be what is most important.

Resources are available to those educators and administrators who want to align their learning goals to college-readiness standards. The American Diploma Project (see www.achieve.org) outlines English and math standards that students should know when they graduate from high school. The Association of American Universities' *Understanding University Success* study (see http://cepr.uoregon.edu/) documents the knowledge and skills that students are expected to have for entry-level university courses in six academic subject areas. David Conley (2005) provides readers with a thorough discussion of what he calls "college knowledge."

All Standards Are Not Unidimensional

A third problem with using existing state standards is what Robert Marzano (2006) calls a lack of unidimensionality. State standards and benchmarks typically mix multiple dimensions (i.e., information and skills) in a single statement which must be "unpacked" to be useful for instructional and assessment purposes. For example, Marzano cites the following 5th-grade benchmark from the National Council of Teachers of Mathematics: *Develop fluency in adding, subtracting, multiplying, and dividing whole numbers* (p. 15).

This benchmark actually encompasses four different mental processes or dimensions, one each for adding, subtracting, multiplying, and dividing. Subject-matter experts need to analyze benchmarks such as this one to identify its separate dimensions as well as to "delete content that is not considered essential, delete content that is not amenable to classroom assessment, and combine content that is highly related" (Marzano & Haystead, 2008, pp. 12–13).

The Same Set of Standards Allows for Different Expectations

The final problem with using state standards as the guaranteed and viable curriculum is that without considerable further definition, the same state standard can be taught and assessed in a different way by different teachers. Paul Bambrick-Santoyo (2007–08) demonstrates the reality of vastly different expectations with six different assessment examples of the same 7th-grade New Jersey state math standard: *Understand and use percents in a variety of situations.*

1. What is 50 percent of 20?
2. What is 67 percent of 81?
3. Shawn got 7 correct out of 10 possible answers on his science test. What percentage of questions did he answer correctly?
4. J. J. Redick was on pace to set a college basketball record in career free throw percentage. Going into the NCAA tournament in 2004, he made 97 of 104 free throw attempts. What percent of free throws had he made?
5. Using the previous example, in the first tournament game, Redick missed his first five free throws. How far did his percentage drop from right before the tournament game to right after missing those free throws?
6. J. J. Redick and Chris Paul were competing for the best free throw percentage. Redick made 94 percent of his first 103 shots, whereas Paul made 47 of 51 shots.
    a. Which one had a better shooting percentage?
    b. In the next game, Redick made only 2 of 10 shots, and Paul made 7 of 10 shots. What are their overall shooting percentages? Who is the better shooter?
    c. Jason argued that if J. J. and Chris each made their next 10 shots, their shooting percentages would go up the same amount. Is

> this true? Why or why not? Describe in detail how you arrived at your answers. (p. 44)

Obviously, teaching to the same state standard does not guarantee consistency.

Balancing the Art and Science of Teaching

Teachers will also use the you're-taking-all-of-the-creativity-out-of-teaching argument. This response will include arguments such as

- "Establishing a guaranteed and viable curriculum is an attack on academic freedom."
- "Thanks for taking the art out of teaching."
- "So, if it's October 17th, you want us all to be on page 86, right?"

Clarifying learning goals through a guaranteed and viable curriculum does not need to lead to "scripted" teaching. Robert Marzano (2007) devotes several paragraphs in *The Art and Science of Teaching* to establish the position that teaching is both an art and a science. He emphatically states, "I strongly believe that there is not (nor will there ever be) a formula for effective teaching" (p. 4). A guaranteed and viable curriculum identifies the "what" of teaching, not the "how." How a particular learning goal will be taught will always require considerable judgment on the part of teachers (the art of teaching), within the guidelines provided by the research on best practices (the science of teaching).

The academic freedom argument is an example of the logical error "appealing to emotion." Freedom of inquiry for students and faculty must be safeguarded, but that inquiry needs to be focused on the learning goals that the school or district has collaboratively determined to be most important. A fellow principal occasionally found it necessary to remind members of his very talented faculty that "you're not self-employed." As a high school principal confronted with the you're-taking-the-creativity-out-of-teaching argument, I occasionally resurrected the prophecy, "We'll never be as good as we can be, or as good as we need to be, as long as the ruling metaphor of the American high school is 'A collection of educational entrepreneurs held together by a common parking lot.'" Reactions to my witticism were mixed.

Michael Fullan (2008) makes an important distinction with regard to this particular dismissive response when he asserts that what we must be about is "the pursuit of *precision, not prescription*" (p. 82). Teachers in highly effective schools know precisely what they are after.

Using Professional Learning Communities to Establish Clear Learning Goals

After educators and leaders have established the importance of focusing instruction and assessment around clear learning goals by developing a guaranteed and viable curriculum, the question becomes, "How are high schools getting it done?" There are different approaches that have common elements which can help you arrive at the same goal.

Using Common Outcomes

Rick and Becky DuFour advocate for what they call the team learning process (DuFour & DuFour, 2004). Although sometimes difficult to put into practice because of structural, cultural, and leadership barriers, the process itself is really quite straightforward and easy to understand. It is as follows:

1. Clarify 8 to 10 essential common outcomes per semester by course or content area
2. Develop at least four common assessments per year
3. Establish specific measurable standards or goals (i.e., SMART goals)
4. Analyze results
5. Identify and implement improvement strategies

The process makes intuitive sense: decide where you're going, establish performance goals, periodically assess students to gauge their progress via those outcomes and goals, look at the results, and do something different in your instructional goals if the results aren't to your liking.

In addition to its simple elegance, what gives this process credibility is the fact that its creators have walked the talk. Becky DuFour used the process with positive results in her elementary school in Virginia and won state and national recognition for her school's implementation of the professional learning community model. Rick DuFour implemented the team learning process while serving as principal at Adlai Stevenson High School outside of Chicago. The teacher collaboration model is still in place there and has helped the staff at Stevenson progress from being just another good suburban high school to becoming an outstanding school. Ninety-six percent of the students at this large and diverse school go to college (Honawar, 2008).

As a speaker at the New Century School Summit in Colorado, Mike Schmoker (2007) said the model proposed by the DuFours is potentially so powerful that if high schools in this country did nothing more than implement that model, we would move to the top of the pack on international assessments for student achievement. Elsewhere, Schmoker describes the success that Johnson City High School in New York had while implementing such a model (DuFour, Eaker, & DuFour, 2005). The school increased the number of students passing the Regents Exam from 47 percent to 93 percent in one year using the process below. The teachers at Johnson City

- Divided essential math skills and knowledge from the Regents Exam into four quarters
- Designed quarterly common assessments for these topics
- Met regularly to prepare, test, and refine lessons and strategies
- Used assessment results to adjust instruction

The Johnson City High School process represents just a slight variation on the DuFour theme. They used different approaches with common elements to arrive at a common goal.

Developing Power Standards and Essential Tasks

Littleton High School in Colorado provides another example of educators and leaders who joined their efforts together to identify learning goals at the building, department, and course level. In the late 1980s and early 1990s, the faculty at Littleton High School began to make the conceptual shift from a focus on seat time (i.e., Carnegie units) to what is known today as standards-based education [formerly known as performance-based education] (National Association of Secondary School Principals, 2004; Westerberg, 2007). The initiative was named Direction 2000 and it identified 19 performance-based graduation requirements and corresponding performance assessments on which all students were expected to demonstrate mastery. The ground-breaking initiative was met with political opposition from a conservative "back-to-basics" parent group before it was fully implemented. But, rather than abandon using performance instead of time as the measure of achievement, the faculty modified the original concept to accommodate a more traditional vision of schooling. Today, learning goals and performance standards are presented and used in power standards and essential tasks.

Writer and researcher Douglas Reeves introduced the concept of using power standards as a method of identifying schoolwide learning goals to the staff at Littleton through a series of presentations to the faculty and administration. In a nutshell, Reeves's argument, as briefly outlined earlier in this chapter, is that schools attempt to cover too many standards and are not doing a good job of teaching any of them. Instead of this frantic attempt at coverage, Reeves recommends that educators identify a smaller number of standards that are especially powerful because of their endurance (i.e., the standard is valuable beyond a single test date), leverage (i.e., the standard is useful in multiple disciplines), and facility for preparing students for the next level of learning (Reeves, 2001). The problem of trying to cover too much material in one school year had an immediate emotional appeal for teachers.

In a yearlong collaborative process that included all of the teachers, administrators, parents, and students at Littleton, the school community identified and later adopted four schoolwide learning goals (or power standards) that the faculty agreed were too important to leave to chance: nonfiction writing, information literacy, citizenship and work habits, and thinking and reasoning. The staff focused on implementing these standards over several years and devoted two to three years to define, clarify, and train faculty members on how to teach and assess each power standard. For example, every teacher at Littleton High School is expected to provide instruction in the writing process in every class every semester using the school's adopted common language and rubric.

The expectations for these power standards at Littleton go well beyond just including a few open-ended questions on a test and giving students grades. Teachers are expected to teach the writing process which includes direct instruction, feedback, peer editing, and revision. Professional development time is used to examine student writing and survey results at both the department level and in cross-disciplinary teams. For students, having this level of direct instruction on nonfiction writing in multiple disciplines using a common language and a common rubric 50, 60, or even 70 times in their high school career is quite powerful!

Contrast that approach with what typically occurs in many American high schools. For almost 100 years at Littleton High School, the de facto posture regarding writing was based on an assumption (or perhaps hope) that students would develop their writing skills as they passed through the curriculum, regardless of the courses they chose and the teachers to whom they were assigned. The elephant in the room at most high schools is that that assumption and similar assumptions about other important knowledge and skills are not valid. Some students are fortunate and determined enough to graduate as strong writers. Others, we know, are not.

Michael Fullan (2008) says, "Successful organizations are 'all over' the practices that are known to make a difference" (p. 77). Highly effective schools leave nothing important to chance. Instead, they are very deliberate about what is essential for students to know and be able to do.

You may not agree with the particular power standards chosen by the Littleton High School community. That's OK. Faculty members there don't care unless you join the staff. In that case, you need to get on board with what constitutes a schoolwide guaranteed curriculum. The goals that are ultimately selected are not as important as the fact that they are collaboratively developed, based on local performance data, and used to advance the school's or district's mission.

The essential tasks that are identified by staff members at Littleton High School constitute, in part, the guaranteed and viable curriculum at the department or course level. For example, the science department has identified *article critique* and *experimental design* as essential tasks. Teachers in the science department feel that in our scientific and technological world, our economic, social, and political systems cannot function effectively unless ordinary citizens are able to critically evaluate a science-related article in publications like *Newsweek* or the *Denver Post.* Likewise, obtaining a thorough understanding of the experimental design process is too central to what scientists do to leave the development of that understanding to chance. Another example comes from the physical education department, where all teachers have committed to focus on cardiovascular fitness as defined by departmentwide performance standards.

Many education experts identify essential standards differently. The DuFours (2004) call them "outcomes," Schmoker refers to them as "essential knowledge and skills," Wiggins and McTighe (2007) label them "understandings," Marzano (2006) prefers "measurement topics," the National Association of Secondary School Principals (2004) uses the term "essential learnings," Reeves (2001) talks about "power standards," and Littleton High School uses a combination of power standards and essential tasks (Westerberg, 2007). Although there are some important differences in these conceptualizations, they can all be used to identify learning goals that serve as the focus for all aspects of instructional planning and implementation. It does not matter what you call them, but it does matter that you identify, articulate, and operationalize them.

Developing Learning Goals at the Classroom Level

We are ready to move now from the big picture learning goals at the course and grade level to setting specific unit objectives at the classroom level. Sometimes, schoolwide learning goals can be readily used as objectives for individual units of instruction. Other times, these goals need to be further broken down or "unpacked" to fit a teacher's approach for a particular set of skills or knowledge. Depending on the characteristics and parameters of a particular learning process the degree of covariance among the elements within the larger goal will dictate how much work teachers must do to move from the guaranteed and viable curriculum to unit objectives.

The following is an example of a learning goal identified by a school district as one of eight major outcomes for second-semester 7th-grade geography: *Students understand the relationship between topography, natural resources, and culture*. This goal could also serve as the primary objective for a two-week unit of instruction. In another example, the following power standard, *Students write and speak effectively for a variety of purposes and audiences using proper conventions*, is probably too encompassing and multidimensional to serve effectively as an individual unit objective.

In either case, a well-supported argument exists for beginning the unit design process by establishing clear learning objectives or goals and communicating them to students early and often. Robert Marzano (2007) reports increases in student achievement ranging from 16 to 41 percentile points in his review of research results on goal setting. In the largest of these studies, when students know what they are supposed to be learning, their performance, on average, increased by 21 percentile points. "Instructional goals narrow what students focus on" (Marzano, Pickering, & Pollock, 2001, p. 94).

Distinguishing Between Learning Activities and Learning Goals

In my visits to high school classrooms, often in highly-acclaimed schools, I frequently find that students know what they are responsible for doing, but not what they are supposed to be learning. If I ask a student, "What are you supposed to be learning by doing _____ (the activity at hand)," he or she responds with a frustrated "I don't know. She just told us to read the chapter and answer the questions at the end." Wrong answer!

There is an important distinction between learning activities and learning goals. "Completing a science lab on osmosis" is not a learning goal nor are "preparing and presenting a report on cocaine," "solving the problems at the end of chapter 7," or "writing an essay." These are learning activities. Learning goals state what students will understand or be able to do as a result of engaging in one or more well-constructed learning activities. Examples of learning goals are as follows: *Understand the relationship among topography, natural resources, and culture, Know the states and their capitals, Revise an essay to improve word choice,* and *Engage in a series of drills to improve dribbling skills.* Marzano (2007) and Wiggins and McTighe (2007) provide more detailed discussions of the distinction between activities and learning goals.

When teachers solely focus on learning activities, this promotes a check-it-off mentality for students. You will hear them say things like, "When is this due?" "How many sources do I have to have?" "How many points is this worth?" "Can I get extra credit for wearing a costume?" or "Just tell me what to do so I can check it off." Many parents witness the check-it-off mentality on a regular basis. When our youngest daughter was in 7th grade, we asked her if she really understood anything she was copying out of her science book and into her notebook. She responded, "I don't care. I just have to get something down so the teacher can check it off." As a 9th grade student, this same daughter was assigned a book to read in her language arts class. The single criterion for getting an *A* seemed to be that the book had to be at least 200 pages in length. One copy of her favorite book, *Seabiscuit,* was 198 pages in length. Borders had another version of the book with different print and 212 pages. This was yet another item to check off.

Our youngest son had summer assignments between his sophomore and junior years in high school in preparation for entering the International Baccalaureate program at his school. The assignments included reading two novels for language arts; completing worksheets in Spanish, chemistry, math, and biology; and reading the first nine chapters in a history book. He was given no guidance regarding what to read or look for as he completed his assignments. He completed the assignments in a mindless fashion, but his teachers checked it off the next fall. Assignments without clear learning goals do not promote learning and amount to no more than busy work for students. Learning goals should help students focus on what is to be learned.

A focus on learning goals rather than performance goals (e.g., scoring proficient on the state test) has been shown to increase student motivation (Jalongo, 2007; Newell & Van Ryzin, 2007). Newell and Van Ryzin (2007) say

> A 'learning' or 'mastery' goal orientation represents a desire to achieve purely for the purpose of obtaining knowledge and increasing skill. A 'performance' or 'ego' goal orientation, on the other hand, represents a focus on appearances rather than on real learning. The perceived goal orientation of a school can significantly affect a student's own goal orientation. Students who perceive that their school exhibits a 'learning' goal orientation seek challenges, show persistence in the face of adversity, use more effective learning strategies, have more positive attitudes, and are more cognitively engaged in learning." (p. 467)

The findings of Newell and Van Ryzin have profound implications for today's test- and performance-driven high schools. It's no wonder students show a lack of interest, engagement, and persistence when the implied or expressed purpose of school is limited to obtaining a certain score on a test. Raising test scores is a necessary and important leadership responsibility, but it is not the purpose of schooling. We must communicate more important goals to students than just raising test scores when they ask, "Why go to school?"

Allowing students to personalize learning goals also enhances student motivation (Marzano, Pickering, & Pollock, 2001). Steffen Saifer and Rhonda Barton (2007) provide an example of how one teacher combined culture and chemistry in a molecular modeling project by asking students to investigate how their molecules might affect their culture or community. Several Chinese students studied the impact of the Opium Wars on their culture, and one black student studied high levels of lactose intolerance among members of the black community.

In *Using Technology with Classroom Instruction That Works*, Pitler and colleagues direct readers to software programs that assist students in personalizing learning goals. The programs help students construct graphic organizers to visually represent the relationship between unit goals and students' individual interests (Pitler, Hubbell, Kuhn, & Malenoski, 2007).

The Principal's Role in Developing a Guaranteed and Viable Curriculum

Kim Marshall (2006) and other leading researchers and authors in the context of standards-based education (DuFour, Eaker, & DuFour, 2005; Schmoker, 2006; Umphrey, 2008) raised the question about the principal's role in developing curriculum several years ago. Marshall's question presupposes that principals are not able to do everything they might like to do to improve teaching and learning in their school; therefore, they have to make choices. Marshall asks readers to pick the three activities that will have the greatest impact on teaching and learning from the following seven options: (1) traditional supervision and evaluation process, (2) walkthroughs, (3) mini-observations with follow-up conversations, (4) quick "drive-by" visits, (5) collecting teachers' lesson plans, (6) requiring teams of teachers to submit common curriculum unit plans with follow-up discussions, and (7) helping teams of teachers analyze and use the results of interim assessments. Marshall's recommendations, based on research results, suggest that I may have wasted at least 10 years of my career.

That last statement is admittedly an exaggeration. In retrospect, however, it seems that I must have spent a decade of my 26 years as a principal in my basement writing lengthy summative evaluation reports as part of the teacher supervision and evaluation process. As I suspected all along, this was definitely not one of those activities on Marshall's list of recommendations. For new and veteran teachers whose continued employment in the district was in question, the process served a legal purpose. For veteran teachers in good standing, however, the process was mostly a game. I pretended to have gained a complete understanding of their strengths and weaknesses as a teacher, and they pretended to be truly enlightened by my observations and recommendations.

Principals who strive to build instruction and learning on a foundation of clearly defined instructional goals should spend their time devoted to instructional leadership or leadership for learning. They also need to be focused on meeting with teams of teachers, reviewing and clarifying learning goals, examining the formative assessments that teachers use to monitor student progress, and asking questions about teachers' intervention plans for struggling students. Principals also need to make time to ask teachers, "What are you trying to accomplish?" "How are the kids doing?" "How do you know when students are not mastering a specific skill?" and "What are you doing to help them improve?"

These are far different foci than that which has occupied high school principals in the past. Notice the emphasis on working mostly with teams of teachers rather than with individuals. For most of my career, my work to improve instruction and learning was a private affair between the teacher and me. These one-on-one sessions unintentionally reinforced the old mental model of teachers working in isolation. Marshall (2008) offers time-management strategies for busy principals who wish to shift their instructional leadership work toward more productive activities. These strategies include adapting a number of mindsets:

- I have a laser-like focus on student achievement and a strategic plan for the year.
- My staff members know exactly what is expected of them in terms of classroom instruction and discipline.
- I have an effective personal planning system for each year, month, week, and day.
- All of my key teams (e.g., leadership, grade-level) are scheduled to meet on a regular basis.
- I have a foolproof system for writing things down, prioritizing and following up.
- I have highly competent people in key roles and delegate maximum responsibility to them.
- I visit 3–5 classrooms a day and give face-to face feedback to each teacher within 24 hours.
- I have effective strategies for preventing or deflecting time-wasting crises and activities.

- I take care of myself, including family, health, exercise, sleep, and vacations.
- I regularly evaluate progress toward my goals and work on continuous improvement.

Of course, this new learning leader role for principals assumes that principals know good instruction when they see it. Doug Reeves reminds us that this necessary precondition is not always in place (2008, April). He says

> To fulfill their instructional leadership role, school administrators have been exhorted to monitor instruction more closely with walk-throughs and other supervisory techniques. But administrators can walk marathons through classrooms of a school and accomplish nothing if they do not begin with a clear conception of what effective instruction looks like. (p. 92)

Having a clear concept of what effective instruction looks like is the subject of the next chapter of this book. The question at this point is, "How are principals spending their time?" Instructional leadership is a precious thing to lose.

Increase the Rigor or Succumb to Rigor Mortis

By closely examining students' required thinking for each unit learning goal, we have a window of opportunity to look into an issue that has become a mantra of school reform in districts across the country—increase the rigor of the curriculum.

Increasing Rigor by Increasing Quality

In newspapers and education publications, there are many accounts from districts and states across the country that are adding quantity to the curriculum and then boasting of having increased rigor. Increasing the number of courses or credits required for graduation, especially in math and science, and encouraging all students to take college-prep courses (or courses with college-prep titles) has become the favorite battle cry among politicians and education reformers alike in the fight against ignorance. For example, since 2001, 33 states have enacted policies that in some way alter graduation requirements, with several of those alterations increasing the number of courses or units required in core areas (*Recent State Policies*, 2007). Colorado is among several states with pending legislation to increase credit-based graduation requirements.

Since 2001, 11 states have decided to begin requiring students to complete a college-prep course sequence (Toch, Jerald, & Dillon, 2007). Similar activities at the district level far outnumber the cases of "increased rigor" as reported by the states.

The results of the quantity approach to defining rigor have been almost universally disappointing, particularly for poor and minority students. *Education Week* (Kennedy-Manzo, 2007) and the *Los Angeles Times* (Landsberg, 2007) recently published articles based on two federal reports which concluded that although high school students are completing a more challenging core curriculum than they were 15 years ago, the scores for seniors in math and reading remain flat or have declined.

In *Education Week*, Kay and Houlihan (2006) note that despite a focus on increasing traditional metrics (e.g., graduation requirements), U.S. students perform poorly not only on the National Assessment of Educational Progress (NAEP) but on tests involving international comparisons as well. The Chicago Public Schools increased its graduation requirements in 1997, but a 2005 *Chicago Tribune* article reported that between 60 and 90 percent of college freshmen failed college placement tests (Toch, Jerald, & Dillon, 2007). Jay Mathews (2006) of the *Washington Post* described a case where "course-label inflation," (i.e., courses that promise more than they deliver) had been particularly harmful to low-income and minority students in Texas when it was time for them to take the required state exam. The College Board has begun an audit of every AP course in the nation in response to concerns that the recent dramatic increase in the number of students taking AP courses may be resulting in more quantity than quality. This audit will help to ensure college leaders that there has been no decrease in the rigor of the program (de Vise, 2007).

The results from the tendency to align rigor with quantity is best summed up by Nel Noddings (2007) from Stanford University. She describes the current effort to increase rigor in schools as a form of mental drudgery that focuses on a few discrete skills and is devoid of intellectual content. Noddings and others call for a new definition of rigor that centers on increasing the quality of the educational experience and develops intellectual habits of mind.

Education writers and researchers are building a consensus around a new definition of rigor that has more to do with quality than with quantity. Noddings (2007) defines rigor as designing work in which students are "asked to identify for themselves the important points in every unit of study, construct their own summaries, attempt problems that have no obvious solutions, engage in interpretation, and evaluate conflicting expectations and points of view" (p. 32). Washor and Mojkowski (2006–07) envision rigor as a learning environment that involves "deep immersion in a subject over time, with learners using sophisticated texts, tools, and language in real-world settings. In such settings, students encounter complex, messy problems for which tools and solutions may not be readily apparent or available" (p. 85). These authors also describe rigorous work as reflective, interactive for students, and open for peer and public scrutiny and opportunities for practitioners to act as mentors. Daniel Baron (2007) offers the following definition for more consideration on rigor:

> Rigor is the goal of helping students develop the capacity to understand content that is complex, and personally or emotionally challenging. In rigorous schools, students are evaluated by how they apply their understanding of content in new and unique situations. (p. 50)

Common themes that run through these and other definitions and descriptions of rigor include problem solving, critical thinking, reflection, ownership, communication, creativity, complexity, breadth and depth, and connections. When we look at rigor based on these definitions, it has very little to do with the quantity of work we assign to students. Instead, it has a great deal to do with the quality of the work we ask students to do and the types of assessments we use to monitor and evaluate student progress.

Creating Rigorous Curricula and Instruction

School or district leaders who are interested in creating curricula and instruction that reflect true rigor can begin to re-evaluate what they are doing by engaging in the following six-step process:

- Begin the conversation with teachers and administrators at the school or district level.
- Identify and analyze available frameworks and models on rigor.
- Test selected frameworks and models for the best fit for the school or district.
- Adapt existing frameworks and models to create a framework for use throughout the school or district.

- Use the adopted framework or model to analyze and modify existing units of instruction.
- Provide systemic support for framework or model.

1. *Begin the conversation.* I often begin my conversations about rigor by adapting a quote by Mark Twain: "Everybody talks about rigor but nobody does anything about it." There are precious few schools and district leaders who are having conversations that are aimed at arriving at a common understanding of rigor.

The first step in creating rigor is to begin the conversation. Faculty and district members can start by using any number of common protocols and identifying and sharing their definitions for rigor. During these conversations, it will soon become evident that each participant defines rigor differently and there will be common themes among the definitions. One tool recommended in *Breaking Ranks II* is the School Academic Rigor & Support Self-Assessment tool. It uses a discrepancy model format, which allows school stakeholders to compare desired and actual levels of 70 interdependent rigor and support characteristics and then analyze results using planning tools that accompany the survey.

2. *Identify and analyze available frameworks and models.* Several conceptual frameworks and models are available to extend and deepen the conversation beyond the awareness level. Grubb and Oakes (2007) offer the following seven conceptions of rigor that provide an excellent foundation for school communities who want to define or describe rigor in their curriculum:

- Rigor as student effort (i.e., more hours of homework equals increased rigor)
- Test-based rigor (i.e., international comparisons, high school exit exams)
- Content-based rigor (i.e., all students must pursue a college-prep program or take an AP class)
- Rigor as breadth versus depth
- Rigor as levels of sophistication (i.e., from decoding to comprehension to analytic judgments about texts)
- Rigor as application and transfer
- Rigor as intellectual breadth (i.e., the well-rounded student) (pp. 12–15)

Grubb and Oakes point out that the standards-based approach to school reform has been almost exclusively focused on test- and content-based rigor. They argue that this focus has very little potential for preparing youth for the economic, civic, and intellectual demands of the 21st century. Instead, they urge us to consider conceptions four through seven as foundations for increasing rigor in our schools.

Willard Daggett, from the International Center for Leadership in Education, offers what he calls a Rigor/Relevance framework as a tool for examining curriculum, instruction, and assessment (*Rigor/Relevance Framework*, n.d.). The framework consists of four quadrants (acquisition, application, assimilation, and adaptation) that include instructional and assessment strategies that are particularly effective in eliciting high levels of student performance. The quadrants are created by plotting five points from an application model on the horizontal axis and six points from Bloom's Taxonomy on the vertical axis of a grid.

Another model I have found useful in helping teachers plan for rigor is Robert Marzano's (2007) comprehensive framework of effective teaching. This framework is presented in the form of 10 instructional design questions. Design question 4 (What will I do to help students generate and test hypotheses about new knowledge?) specifically addresses the issue of rigor. Some of the strategies listed for generating and testing hypotheses include teaching students how to effectively support a claim, engage in experimental inquiry, solve problems, make decisions, and investigate learning tasks. Activities like these address the common themes that run through the more enlightened definitions and descriptions of rigor just presented. The Education Trust also has a model for evaluating rigor called Standards in Practice (SIP). SIP is a six-step professional development model that focuses on increasing instructional rigor.

External benchmarks can be important resources in helping educators evaluate the rigor of local instruction. For example, Byram Hills High School in Armonk, New York, uses the Intel Science Talent Search competition as a model for instilling rigor into teaching and learning. This competition is a rich learning experience that includes many of the descriptors of rigorous instruction outlined here. Each year, nearly a quarter of the sophomore class at Byram Hills signs up to do research (Berger, 2007).

The content and performance standards from programs such as Intel, International Baccalaureate, and High Schools That Work can be used to calibrate the level of rigor for instruction.

3. *Test selected frameworks and models.* At this point, it is a good idea to try out a few frameworks and models to give teachers a feel for how they work when they are applied to sample units of instruction. During this period, you are looking for a good fit between the framework and your school's or district's philosophy and belief systems. Rigor will not move from the conference room to the classroom unless teachers believe that the framework helps to increase rigor in the classroom.

4. *Adapt existing frameworks and models for use throughout the school or district.* After you have tested a few frameworks, you are now ready to adopt a local framework or model to guide the ongoing examination of curricular and instructional rigor at the school or district level. It is seldom that school leaders will adopt an existing framework or model as a whole. Key players, however, will pick parts of an existing framework or model that align with the school's or district's belief systems and add any elements they believe are missing. The adopted framework or model must be written and widely disseminated and discussed.

The Adams 50 School District in Westminster, Colorado, has developed a working definition of rigor, along with supporting statements that describe what rigorous teaching and rigorous learning look like in practice. The Adams model, shown in Figure 3.1, reflects characteristics of several of the aforementioned frameworks and models.

5. *Use the adopted framework or model to analyze and modify existing units of instruction.* Teachers can gain a deep understanding of and fidelity for a new framework or model when they use the framework to analyze and modify existing units of instruction. At the elementary level, implementing a new framework can be done in grade-level teams, and at the secondary level, course or department teams may be more appropriate. For example, the assignments in Figures 3.2 and 3.3 could be compared with regard to rigor by using a newly adopted framework or model. This kind of collaborative work fits perfectly with the professional learning community (PLC) model supported by research (DuFour, Eaker, & DuFour, 2005; National Association of Secondary School Principals, 2004; Schmoker, 2006) and with increasing popularity in schools.

Figure 3.1
Rigor Definitions from the Adams 50 School District

Administrators' Definition of Rigor
Rigor is an expectation that students will demonstrate success with consistent high standards for academic achievement and behavioral excellence through multiple, relevant learning opportunities.

Teachers' Definition of Rigor
Academic rigor is the quality or action that requires an individual to challenge oneself to persevere in order to increase one's complexity of knowledge and thinking and perform at a higher level.

RIGOROUS LEARNING	RIGOROUS TEACHING
How do we know rigorous learning when we see it? • Students are focused on performance targets and know how to achieve them • Know and demonstrate an understanding of expectations, objectives, and standards • Students can articulate purpose of learning • Students know why it's important to learn goals • More student-to-student talk • Engaged in authentic work • Self-motivated • On task • Ownership and responsibility for own learning • Classroom is interactive • Interaction with content through questioning, dialogue, cooperative learning, research • Persistence and resilience = risk taking • Ask questions and apply knowledge and higher–level thinking • Challenged to think • Extracurricular challenges as well as classes • Reflection of learning experience through projects, journaling, and talking • Expression of new insights on own progress • System access to high-level course work with support • New level of performance • Application of knowledge transferring to other situations	**What does rigorous teaching look like?** • Clearly communicating learning objective and expectations of performance proficiency • Insists on reaching the learning goal • Expectations and belief in each student's success • ALWAYS challenging students' thinking • Moving students toward being lifelong independent learners • Building student capacity • All students can participate and contribute to the classroom learning • Engage the student actively and authentically • Appropriate balance of knowledge/skill/application • Higher-level questioning • Progressive questioning (What's next…?) • Evidence of reflection, self-evaluation, analyzing • Ongoing assessment to increase complexity of learning • Evidence of a classroom environment that leads from teacher-directed to learner-directed • Good collaboration (Teacher to Student, Teacher to Teacher, Student to Student) • Relevancy • Documented topics, skills, planned order • Materials need to fit the challenge (appropriate materials; evidence of thoughtful planning to lead to learning goals) • Teaching Learning Cycle effectively (Curriculum, instruction, assessment, evaluation) • In-depth study of essential learnings • Cross-curricular integration

Source: Adams 50 School District, Westminster, CO. Reprinted with permission.

Figure 3.2

Sample Assignment Using Rigor

This project requires that you find information, write a report, make a display, and give an oral presentation.

Select a state that you would enjoy studying. Find information about your state that will help us understand what it is like to live there. You might include the state symbols, the flag, the geography, the way people make their living, or the animals that live there.

Write a report that describes your state. Make a poster that displays important information that you will use as you present your information to the class.

On your assigned day, you will present your information. Be sure to practice and speak clearly to the class. You should also wear something that symbolizes the state. (You may bring food that is typical of the state to share with the class for five extra credit points.)

You will be evaluated as follows:

- Information — 15 points
  - Important information
  - Recorded on note cards
- Report — 30 points
  - Well-organized
  - Typed
- Display — 20 points
  - Colorful and creative
- Oral presentation — 20 points
  - Organized
  - Good eye-contact, loud voice
  - Dressed in clothes that symbolize the state

Extra Credit? — 5 points

TOTAL ____________ out of 90

Source: D. Pickering, Littleton, CO. Reprinted with permission.

Figure 3.3
Sample Assignment Using Rigor with Rubrics

Exploring Topography, Natural Resources, and Culture

1. Select a state or country that interests you.

2. During our computer lab time, find at least two Internet sites that have information about your state and country.

3. Find specific information about that state or country that describes its topography, natural resources, and culture.

4. Through a written or oral report with accompanying visuals or a graphic representation with written explanations, explain how specific aspects of the topography and natural resources influence the culture of the area.

   The goal of this assignment is to make connections between topography, natural resources, and culture. The major connections we have been studying have been focused on how topography and natural resources influence culture, but you might find ways that culture can influence topography and natural resources.

5. On the day that the project is due, you will have two responsibilities. First, you will spend time at your desk and explain the connections to your classmates who are "making the rounds" through the projects. Second, when it is your turn to make the rounds, you will try to learn about connections from five other states or countries that your classmates will be explaining.

(continued)

Figure 3.3 (*Continued*)

Sample Assignment Using Rigor with Rubrics

Rubrics for Exploring Topography, Natural Resources, and Culture

	Understanding the Concepts
4	Demonstrates IN-DEPTH understanding of the relationships; numerous, accurate connections are made and clearly explained; some connections are beyond the types of connections discussed in class. The student also found some examples of how culture can influence topography and natural resources.
3	Demonstrates SOLID, COMPLETE understanding; many connections are made and clearly explained; there are good examples of the types of connections discussed in class.
2	Demonstrates SOMEWHAT LIMITED, understanding; few connections are accurate.
1	Demonstrates an INCOMPLETE, VERY LIMITED understanding; almost no connections were made or there were no explanations.

	Internet Access
4	Can access information from the Internet easily and efficiently.
3	Can access information from the Internet without any significant hesitation.
2	Can access information from the Internet only after false starts and hesitation.
1	Cannot access information from the Internet.

	Presentation
4	The presentation of the information and the accompanying visuals are clear; the words and visuals work together and the major points, with the supporting examples, are clearly connected. The display makes it easy to see the connections.
3	The presentation of the information and the accompanying visuals are clear; the words and picture show the connections and there are supporting examples for the major points.
2	The presentation of the information and the accompanying visuals are clear; there are words and visuals, but it is hard to make the connections between them. The major points are not supported with examples.
1	The presentation of the information and the accompanying visuals are not clear.

Figure 3.3 (*Continued*)

Sample Assignment Using Rigor with Rubrics

Teacher's Evaluation for Topography, Natural Resources, Culture

Name: ______________________________ Date:______________

Learning Goals:	Feedback:			
1. Understand the relationships among concepts of topography, natural resources, and culture	1	2	3	4 (see rubric)
2. Access information from the Internet	1	2	3	4 (see rubric)
3. Present information, using visuals	1	2	3	4 (see rubric)

Source: D. Pickering, Littleton, CO. Reprinted with permission.

6. *Ensure that the system supports the framework or model.* A study of national policy and research organizations by the National Alliance of High Schools (Housman, Muller, & Chait, 2006) identified the following four themes with regard to strategies for increasing academic rigor:

- Raising graduation requirements
- Ensuring access to quality course content and instruction
- Aligning course content and assessments with the skills necessary for higher education and employment
- Institutionalizing additional support for students at risk (pp. 2–5)

The approach to rigor that I have described thus far has focused on aligning curriculum and instruction with the 21st century demands of higher education and employment. However, care must be taken to ensure that rigor is not unintentionally sabotaged by other parts of the system. For example, increasing rigor without providing additional support for at-risk students could be a prescription for disaster. As is true with most significant school improvement efforts, thinking about the whole system is necessary.

Purposeful conversations about defining rigor need to be happening in every school and district in the country. This conversation isn't just a high school conversation. The notion that developing intellectual habits of mind can begin in high school is naive at best. Research and common sense tell us that rigorous learning experiences are good for students at all levels. Without these conversations and a willingness to use a structured process to act on the shared understandings reached through them, millions more American students each year will display the disturbing signs of educational rigor mortis and the life of education will be gone from them forever.

Establishing and communicating clear instructional goals and using state standards as a beginning point is the antidote to curriculum anarchy. It is also the first step in becoming a great high school. Highly effective high schools are very precise about what they intend to accomplish, and they know how to move beyond a focus on instructional activities to a focus on rigorous instructional goals. Instructional leadership in these schools looks very different from what has traditionally been the norm. This type of leadership is focused on discussions with teams of teachers about common learning goals, formative assessments, and interventions.

4

Strategy 2: Developing a Common Vision of Effective Instruction

If we accept the theory that significant school improvement depends first, last, and foremost on improving the quality of instruction in classrooms, then we should follow up that theory with conversations about effective instructional practices. The catch is that we cannot have an in-depth conversation about effective instruction if we do not share a common language. Each high school community must identify and institutionalize an instructional model that defines and provides a common language for what constitutes effective classroom practice.

Improving a Weak Instructional Core

Richard Elmore (2003) is one of many researchers who highlights the importance of moving from what he calls a weak instructional core to a language of instruction. He says

> Successful leaders understand that improving school performance requires transforming a fundamentally weak instructional core, and the culture that surrounds it into a strong, explicit body of knowledge about powerful teaching and learning that is accessible to those who are willing to learn it. (p. 9)

A weak instructional core is what you have when members of a learning community do not talk about, cannot agree on, or even deny the existence of the science of teaching. It often manifests itself in a culture that conveys the following message to new faculty members:

> Look, teaching is an art, not a science. There is no one right way, or for that matter 'best ways,' to teach (fill in the subject matter). Therefore, what I do in my classroom is my business and what you do in your classroom is your business. After all, teaching is an art, not a science.

Nearly all discussions on professionalism include a specialized body of knowledge and agreed upon standards of practice as the essential characteristics or elements of a profession (Wiggins & McTighe, 2006; Wurtzel, 2006). Professionals who do not have these essential characteristics are at the mercy of outsiders who fill in these quality control gaps. Elmore says (2003)

> Educators are subjected to draconian and dysfunctional external accountability policies largely because they have failed to develop strong and binding professional norms about what constitutes high-quality teaching practice and a supportive educational environment. Internal coherence around instructional practice is a prerequisite for strong performance. (p. 8)

Wurtzel (2007) also weighed in on this hallmark of professionalism and says

> When student performance is weak, student mobility is high, or when teacher expertise is low, teachers are particularly rigorous about using agreed-upon practices to accelerate learning and ensure consistency for students. The use and improvement of effective, evidence-based tools and practices become the hallmarks of instruction. (p. 3)

Many researchers have documented significant variations in the quality of teaching and expectations for students, not only across schools but also across classrooms in the same school (Fullan, 2006; Marzano, 2007; Pianta, 2007; Wereschagin, 2007). Jonathan Supovitz, senior researcher at the Consortium for Policy Research in Education at the University of Pennsylvania, warns education leaders of the price that students pay when they fail to identify and institutionalize an instructional model and language of instruction. One of his recommendations for district-based reform is to develop a clear vision of instructional quality in the major content areas. Supovitz (2007) explains

> Substantial research and craft knowledge exist about what practices are more effective than others, and what practices can be advantageously used for students at particular developmental levels and in particular contextual situations. Educational leaders who do not use this knowledge to develop a clear vision of what instruction should look like—and then enact that vision in their schools—are virtually ensuring uneven quality and effectiveness. (p. 27)

In order for educators to have significant school improvement, professionalism, quality control, effectiveness, and meaningful conversations about teaching and learning, they must demand a clear vision of effective classroom practice and an agreed upon language of instruction.

Developing a Language of Instruction

There are many choices for school and district leaders who wish to adopt and adapt a research-based framework of effective teaching (Fisher & Frey, 2008; Marzano, 2007; Marzano, Pickering, & Pollock, 2001; Reeves, 2008; Wiggins & McTighe, 1998).

The Fisher and Frey model (2008) provides teachers with a framework for what the authors call "the gradual release of responsibility." Within this framework, teachers move through a progression of instructional strategies that include focus lessons ("I do it"), guided instruction ("We do it"), collaborative learning ("You do it together"), and independent tasks ("You do it alone"). These strategies correspond to increasing levels of student responsibility for learning. This model is well suited for a school or district that is focused on developing independent learners.

In *Classroom Instruction That Works*, Marzano and colleagues (2001) identify nine research-based classroom instructional practices that have a proven track record for increasing student achievement when used strategically by skilled teachers. In addition to the research that defines and supports each strategy, the authors provide practical guidelines for classroom implementation. This model works best when unfolded over a period of two or three years. This approach gives teachers time to develop a thorough understanding of each strategy along with opportunities for job-embedded demonstration lessons, guided practice, feedback, and peer coaching. Robert Marzano (2007) recently developed a comprehensive framework for effective teaching (described in detail later in this chapter) that incorporates the nine strategies from *Classroom Instruction That Works* into 10 design questions. Teachers and administrators interested in improving classroom instruction by working to build effective units of instruction are advised to learn more about this model.

In *The New Framework for Teacher Leadership*, Doug Reeves (2008) offers a model for instructional decision making. This model consists of seven elements that begin with the recognition of a challenge and proceeds through a continuous cycle that includes action research, reflection, reinforcement, and resilience. As the name suggests, this instructional decision-making model puts the teacher at the center of ongoing school improvement efforts.

Understanding by Design (UbD) (Wiggins & McTighe, 1998) is more of a curriculum than an instructional model. This model is based on a backward design process for designing curriculum, assessment, and instruction that is focused on big ideas and essential questions. UbD can effectively serve as a common language of instruction for a school or district faculty members. This process appeals to educators interested in moving students beyond knowing to understanding.

Several schools in the Littleton, Colorado, school district adopted the nine strategies identified by Marzano and colleagues (2001) as their language of instruction. For example, teachers in a particular school could talk about how the following strategy, generating and testing hypotheses, could be incorporated into a unit on sources of energy. These teachers can have this conversation because they share a common language embodied in an adopted framework for effective classroom instruction.

Marzano (2007) synthesized his 35 years of educational research on instructional and classroom management strategies and designed 10 instructional design questions that form a comprehensive framework for effective teaching (see Figure 4.1).

Upon further examination, the framework has an internal logic in its sequence of questions that is consistent with the strategies presented in this book. First, an individual teacher or a team of teachers would begin designing a unit of instruction by identifying the unit learning goals, communicating the goals, tracking student progress, and celebrating success (Question 1). From there, teacher-designers would determine the best strategies to help students interact with and deepen their understanding of the content (Questions 2–4), engage students in learning (Question 5), establish and maintain a productive classroom learning environment (Questions 6–8), and maintain high expectations for student achievement (Question 9). Design Question 10 helps teachers combine individual lessons into a cohesive unit of instruction.

Figure 4.1
Instructional Design Questions

1. What will I do to establish and communicate learning goals, track student progress, and celebrate success?
2. What will I do to help students effectively interact with new knowledge?
3. What will I do to help students practice and deepen their understanding of new knowledge?
4. What will I do to help students generate and test hypotheses about new knowledge?
5. What will I do to engage students?
6. What will I do to establish or maintain classroom rules and procedures?
7. What will I do to recognize and acknowledge adherence and lack of adherence to classroom rules and procedures?
8. What will I do to establish and maintain effective relationships with students?
9. What will I do to communicate high expectations for all students?
10. What will I do to develop effective lessons organized into a cohesive unit?

Source: *The Art and Science of Teaching* (p. 7), by R. Marzano, 2007, Alexandria, VA: ASCD. Reprinted with permission.

Models such as these are often adapted to fit the context of a specific team, department, school, or district. When teachers and administrators internalize such a model, this helps them to focus their conversations on a common vision of effective instruction and a common language of instruction.

Confronting Common Practice

Even in the best high schools, common sense and common practice do not always travel together. Traditional teaching norms such as autonomy, egalitarianism, and deference to authority work against conversations in schools about effective instructional practices (Johnson & Donaldson, 2007). Autonomy reveals itself when teachers have a just-let-me-go-in-my-classroom-and-leave-me-alone attitude. Egalitarianism is the practice of behaving as if all teachers are equally skilled. No one is any better or any worse than anyone else and there is little to learn from one another. Deference to seniority is self-explanatory. Senior teachers teach upper-level classes and are presumed to be beyond questioning instructional effectiveness. The concept of a professional learning community does not play well in cultures like these.

Michael Fullan (2006), with his usual adroitness in analyzing school cultures, notes the following observation by E. Campbell:

> Despite all the talk of professional learning communities, one of the most entrenched norms of collegiality is one that equates the ethical treatment of colleagues with a kind of unquestioned loyalty, group solidarity, and an essential belief that teachers as professionals should not interfere in the business of other teachers, criticize them or their practices, or expose their possibly negligent or harmful behavior, even at the expense of students' well-being. (p. 209)

In an analysis of research conducted for the Aspin Institute Program, Wurtzel (2007) concludes

> The use of common tools—whether common student tasks, a core curriculum, common grading rubrics, or formative assessments—runs headlong into common conceptions of teacher professionalism. In high schools in particular, teacher professionalism is often defined primarily as autonomy—the freedom to make decisions about what, how, and sometimes even whom to teach. (p. 3)

Other education researchers have created a consensus around solutions for autonomy, egalitarianism, and deference to seniority as well. Michael Fullan (2006) advises, "The more you de-privatize teaching in a purposeful way, the more you improve teaching, learning and student achievement" (p. 56). The qualifier "in a purposeful way" is critical. When we force teachers into groups and tell them to collaborate, this exercise often results in little more than frustration and cynicism. To be productive, members of collaborative groups need a clear understanding of the product expected at the end of a given period, effective leadership, and protocols with which to conduct their business. Using her trademark humor, Bertice Berry (2004), a noted sociologist, author, lecturer, and educator, sums it up this way: "Inbreeding does not give rise to genius." We must do more, Berry explains, than simply reflect on the effectiveness of the instructional approaches we employ.

Carrie Leana, the Gordon H. Love professor of organization and management at the University of Pittsburgh's Katz Graduate School of Business, summarized the results of a study involving the Pittsburgh Public Schools and suggests that one of the best things schools and districts can do to boost student achievement is to give teachers a chance to talk. Leana found that students in schools in which teachers talked to each other earned significantly higher reading and math test scores than similar schools where teacher talk was not the norm. These communication networks, as Leana labels them, had a bigger impact on student achievement than faculty experience or academic credentials (Roth, 2007). A 2005 research review by the Center for Public Education showed that professional development in high-performing schools is team based and focused on changing instructional practices. In a study of schools that beat the odds, the American Institutes for Research concluded that teachers in such schools were deliberately engaged in collaboration around issues of instructional importance (Hirsh & Killion, 2008).

Patrick Bassett (2008) examined factors that contributed to the success of Finnish schools on tests of international comparisons. He reports

> A second place where American education falls short, in both its public and private segments, is in "professionalizing the profession." While there is much talk about and some progress in creating "professional learning communities" of teachers, and also some promise in creating digital communities, as a country we fall far short of the commitments of our competitors in the world marketplace. (p. 28)

In a joint statement given by the heads of the American Association of School Administrators, the National Association of Secondary School Principals, and the National Board for Professional Teaching Standards, Paul Houston, Gerald Tirozzi, and Joseph Aguerrebere (2007) issued the following statement:

> Rather than being places where teachers work in isolation, schools must promote collaborative work environments in which the expertise of the entire faculty is pooled and the knowledge and skills of the strongest teachers influence all teachers—benefiting all students, not just the select few lucky enough to be assigned to the most effective members of the faculty. (p. 28)

Schools and districts are finding creative ways to provide time for these kinds of collaborative efforts. The following strategies identified in the Principal's Research Review (NASSP, 2004) can help teachers collaborate more effectively:

- Eliminating teacher duty periods.
- Using faculty meeting time for instructional rather than administrative purposes.

- Redistributing professional development days into shorter more frequent meeting times.
- Allowing teachers to have common lunch periods.
- Giving teachers flex time to allow them to arrive at different times and engage in before- or after-school meetings.
- Providing substitute teachers for released time.
- Providing early dismissals or late starts.
- Allowing all students from a team of teachers or department to meet with specialists while core teacher teams work together. (p. 6)

In addition to these strategies, most of which have been or are being employed at Littleton High School in Colorado, I would advocate for adding money to the budget to pay teams of teachers a fair stipend for well-structured summer work.

Like it or not, we'll never be as good as we can be, as long as the ruling metaphor for the American high school is "a collection of educational entrepreneurs held together by a common parking lot." Does your school share an explicit body of knowledge about what constitutes effective teaching?

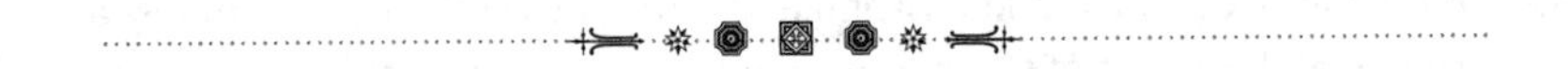

The second essential strategy for becoming a high-performing high school—an unrelenting, collaborative focus on effective instruction—gets at the heart of the business of education. Schools must move from a culture based on autonomy, egalitarianism, and deference to seniority to one that is guided by a research-based framework for effective classroom instruction, a common language of instruction, teamwork, and collaboration.

5

Strategy 3: Using Frequent Formative Assessment

To err may be human, but giving corrective feedback is divine.
—*Janet Metcalf*

With this quotation, Janet Metcalf, a professor of psychology, neurobiology, and behavior at Columbia University, captures the essence of the research on the power of formative assessment (Viadero, 2006). As a principal, few things frustrated me more than hearing a teacher say something to the effect of "I thought the students were getting it. I asked if there were any questions and no one raised their hand, but I just graded the unit exam and there are a lot of *D*s and *F*s. Oh well, on to the next topic."

Assessment used in this way does little to encourage students to keep trying. In fact, this kind of assessment produces a negative rather than a positive response to results. When students receive assessment scores after it is too late to improve their performance, they are not able to accept their roles as data-based instructional decision makers. Rick Stiggins (2008) calls this concept academic self-efficacy. He says, "It is time to replace the intimidation of accountability as our prime motivator with the promise of academic success for all learners as that motivational force" (p. 10).

In a recent e-mail exchange regarding effective feedback, John Hattie, a professor at the University of Auckland and a highly regarded education researcher wrote, "Feedback is one of the most powerful influences [on learning and achievement]—and [it is] surprisingly absent from many classrooms despite the claims by most teachers" (J. Hattie, personal communication, 2008). He argues that feedback needs to fill the gaps between what students understand and what they should aim to understand.

The Power of Feedback

In *The Power of Feedback* (Hattie & Timperley, 2007), John Hattie and co-researcher Helen Timperley reported on a synthesis of over 500 meta-analyses involving 450,000 effect sizes from 180,000 studies. The report included 20 to 30 million students and incorporated more than 100 factors influencing student achievement. The studies in the meta-analyses focused on a wide range of school, home, student, teacher, and curricular attributes that influence student achievement. The average effect size of schooling in this synthesis was 0.40. Effect size is a standardized measure of effect for formative assessment when it is used in meta-analyses where different scales are employed in the individual studies being combined. The larger the effect size, the greater the impact of the intervention. Generally, an effect size of 0.5 is considered large, 0.3 moderate, and 0.1 small. An effect size of 1.0 can be interpreted to mean that a student who scored at the 50th percentile in the control group will be at approximately the 84th percentile or one standard deviation above the mean in the experimental group. For example, the average effect size for studies that included feedback as an influential factor was 0.79. This is nearly twice the average effect size for socioeconomic influences (0.44) and more than six times greater than the average effect size for the number of students per class (0.12). Feedback was ranked in the top 10 highest influential factors (out of more than 100) for student achievement (p. 83).

Also included in *The Power of Feedback* is a synthesis on the effects of feedback from Hattie's massive 1999 database. The findings were as follows:

- Effect sizes were higher when students received feedback about a task and how to do it more effectively. Lower effect sizes were related to praise, rewards, and punishment. (p. 84)
- Feedback is more effective for students when they are given feedback on correct responses instead of on incorrect responses and have information that will help them build on changes from previous trials. (p. 85)
- Feedback has the greatest impact for students when the goals are specific and challenging but the task complexity is low. (pp. 85–86)

In constructing a model for feedback, Hattie and Timperley (2007) begin with the premise that the main purpose of feedback is to reduce the discrepancies between a student's current understandings and performance and a future goal. In their model, teachers and students focus on the answers to the following three questions:

- Where am I going? (i.e., what are my goals?)
- How am I going to get there? (i.e., what progress am I making toward the goal?)
- Where am I going next? (i.e., what activities do I need to undertake to make better progress?)

They refer to the answer for these questions as the "feed up," "feed back," and "feed forward," respectively (p. 87). In another study, Hattie (1999) concludes, "The most powerful innovation that enhances achievement is feedback. The simplest prescription for improving education must be 'dollops of feedback'" (p. 9).

Black and Wiliam (1998) are also frequently cited for their research on the impact of formative assessment on student achievement. In their analysis on feedback, they reported an average effect size of 0.70, which is similar to the impact reported by Hattie (0.79). Black and Wiliam help us gain an understanding of the strength of the relationship between effective feedback and student learning with the following comparison:

> As an illustration of just how big these gains are, an effect size of 0.70, if it could be achieved on a nationwide scale, it would be equivalent to raising the mathematics attainment score of an 'average' country like England, New Zealand, or the United States into the 'top five' after the Pacific rim countries of Singapore, Korea, Japan and Hong Kong. (p. 61)

Rick Stiggins (2008), who is often regarded as the father of the current formative assessment movement, has summarized research on formative assessment and says

> Research evidence gathered in studies conducted literally around the world over the past two decades shows that the consistent application of principles of assessment *for* learning can give rise to profound gains in student achievement, especially for perennial low achievers. (p. 9)

The research of Michael Fullan, Douglas Reeves, Mike Schmoker, and Rick DuFour also supports formative assessment as a catalyst for school improvement (DuFour, 2008). Clearly a case has been made for the argument that frequent formative assessment is one of the most powerful tools high schools can have in their instructional toolkits.

Several high schools in the country have made a commitment to provide effective feedback to students in a systematic way. The Jenks Public Schools in Oklahoma worked with author and consultant Lee Jenkins to identify essential learnings for each of their courses. Their essential learnings were based on state and national standards and incorporated corresponding quizzes that included both review and preview terms. Teachers administered the quizzes on a biweekly basis. After teachers examined the results, they could either design initial instruction with these data or reteach important knowledge and skills (Glandon, personal communication, 2008). The effective use of formative assessment in high school classrooms is more the exception than the rule. So, how do we move from research to practice?

Using Formative Assessment in the Classroom

Rick Stiggins (2008) believes that it is imperative for educators to rethink the role of formative assessment in the classroom based on the changing mission of public education and policymakers' need to understand how formative assessment affects student achievement. He says

> I believe that we have reached a tipping point in the evolution of our schools when we must fundamentally re-evaluate, redefine, and redesign assessment's role in the development of effective schools. The work to be done is so crucial as to require urgent pedagogical, social, and political action. (p. 2)

There is evidence suggesting that policymakers need a new understanding of formative assessment. Commercial publishers are generating half a billion dollars a year in revenue on products labeled as "formative assessment," yet many of these products do not meet the criteria for formative assessment as identified by researchers. In fact, Stiggins has shifted to using the phrase "assessment for learning," and argues that "formative assessment isn't something you buy—it's something you practice" (Cech, 2008, September 17, p. 15).

Before we move on to what formative assessment looks like in the high school classroom, it will be helpful for us to have a definition. James Popham's

(2008) definition for formative assessment reflects a general agreement with other education specialists and aligns with the major tenets of the concept. He defines it as "a planned process in which teachers or students use assessment-based evidence to adjust what they're currently doing" (p. 6). Let's briefly analyze the key components of this definition.

Using a Planned Process with Assessment-Based Evidence

Formative assessment is a process, not a test, although tests may be part of the process. It would not be accurate to say, "I'm giving students a formative test." As Popham explains, it is not the nature of the test that makes it formative but how the test results will be used.

This process is planned, not spontaneous, and it is based on what Popham calls learning progressions. In Popham's scheme, a learning progression consists of "the step-by-step building blocks students are presumed to need in order to successfully attain a more distant, designated instructional outcome" (Popham, 2008, p. 24). In the planning process, teachers build in formal and informal assessments that are designed to provide evidence of students' grasp of things. These assessments will help teachers discover what students need to learn along the way in order to master an important learning goal.

Making Adjustments in Teachers' Instructional Strategies

A primary purpose of formative assessment is to enable teachers to make adjustments in their instructional strategies. Evidence suggests that when teachers are not actively using formative assessment, students are not learning key concepts or skills in a learning progression. Using this information helps to make the process formative.

Making Adjustments in Students' Learning Tactics

Teachers do not act alone in the learning process. Sometimes, students need to use their metacognitive skills and make adjustments in their learning tactics to help them grasp essential content or skills. Practice problems, graphic organizers, summarizing strategies, note taking, and reciprocal teaching are just a few of the research-based strategies that successful students use.

Marzano and colleagues (2001) offer high school educators four concrete research-based recommendations for capitalizing on the potential of effective feedback.

1. *Feedback should be "corrective" in nature.* Marking items right or wrong on assessments does not produce new learning. In order to aid a student's learning process, feedback must help the learner know how to get better next time, or in the words of Hattie and Timperley (2007), feedback must help learners reduce the discrepancies between their current understanding and performance and the learning goal. Stiggins (2004) argues, "We must build classroom environments in which students use assessments to understand what success looks like and how to do better next time" (p. 25).

2. *Feedback should be timely.* Performance information that arrives two semesters, two months, or two weeks after an assessment is administered does little to help the teacher or the student adjust learning strategies in time to correct knowledge or performance discrepancies. When state assessment results from the previous school year are delivered to schools the following fall, they help school leaders to hold themselves accountable, but these results do nothing to increase student learning. Quarterly benchmark assessments may help teachers improve instruction for the *next* group of students, but perhaps with the exception of skills taught over an entire year or semester, these assessments do not help the students who completed the two-week unit on systems of equations last month.

Marzano (2006) summarized the research of Bangert-Drowns and colleagues in his book *Classroom Assessment and Grading That Works*. They focused their research on the correlation between gains in academic achievement and the frequency of assessments over a 15-week period. As expected, the learning curve is quite steep at first, with student achievement increasing by 13.5 percentile points after the first assessment. With successive assessments, the rate of growth levels off, but the students in this study still gained 29.0 percentile points after 30 assessments. Fifteen-week units of instruction are neither the norm nor the recommendation; however, this research does support frequent formative assessment. Teachers can consider implementing formative assessment as often as two or more times per week depending on the students and the nature of the learning goal.

3. *Feedback should be specific to a criterion.* This recommendation is closely tied to the first recommendation. When teachers provide students with the correct answers to questions or performance prompts, students gain a slight increase in learning. When students understand the criteria used to score or judge performance, they have moderate increases in their academic performance (Marzano, 2006).

4. *Students can effectively provide their own feedback.* When teachers build frequent formative assessment into their classroom curriculum design, this process should not become a paper nightmare. Formative assessment can be informal (e.g., interviews, observations, classroom questioning) as well as formal. Students can be taught to assess their own progress toward a learning goal when they are given clear criteria in the form of a rubric or scoring scale.

Figures 5.1 and 5.2 show common examples of the types of feedback that many high school students receive. Given what we know about effective feedback, how do these examples stack up?

In my conversations with hundreds of high school teachers, the majority report that these kinds of examples are closer to the rule than the exception. In Figure 5.1, this student received raw scores without any indication of the criteria used to judge the work or further instructions on how to write a better paper or deliver a better oral report the next time. This student does not know what he needs to do to move from an 80 to a 90 on his next paper. In fact, this student does not even know how to repeat his present level of performance. He is left wondering, "What did I do to score a 75 on the oral report? Maybe I just got lucky." There is one bit of feedback in Figure 5.1 that is "corrective" in nature. The student has learned that he can get 10 extra points by double spacing the next paper. But, is perfecting the art of "space-ology" the intended learning goal? Probably not.

Similarly, analytic scoring formats that are broken down into subcategories, such as sentence structure, mechanics, content, and transitions, can appear to provide the learner with more corrective feedback. However, this type of feedback still does not give students any guidance on how to improve. For example, how does a student know what she needs to do to move from a 6 to a 10 on sentence structure or what she did to score 10 out of 10 on transitions?

Figure 5.2 does provide the learner with specific feedback on her writing, but the feedback does not match the learning goal. Frequent formative

Figure 5.1
Example of Ineffective Feedback for a Student Essay

Double Space!

-10

Oral - 75
Written - 80
155

Ms. [redacted]

Cold War Tensions- US and USSR
The Arms and Space Race

During the stressful times of the Cold War, the United States was faced with a variety of conflicts with the USSR. One main reason that the United States and the Soviet Union were in a Cold War was because of the tensions regarding the Space Race. The Space Race was a competition to see who could create a space exploration program. This impacted the United States not only because there was a need for technological advances in space, but there was also an increase in government spending. The Space Race led the United States to an increased level of nationalism, creating a general opinion of superiority over the Soviet Union. The Soviet Union launched a satellite, Sputnik, which orbited the earth for two months. The satellite created a fear in the United States because Americans believed that it was a spy craft. The United States and the Soviet Union not only had a conflict regarding the space program, but they also were competing to gain a superiority involving nuclear weapon strength. Initially the two super powers, were equal in nuclear power, but each country kept constantly gaining more power than the other. The United States had an entire group of specialists dedicated completely to work on advancements in nuclear technology. Espionage was frequently used by the United States as a key factor in gaining information on advances in the Soviet Union nuclear weapons. The United States began to think of ways to avoid total destruction by nuclear weapons. Underground bunkers were created for those of great importance, and citizens were told to create their own shelters. American citizens were also taught how to act under a nuclear attack. More on the Soviet side, the USSR had yet another success by sending Yuri Gagarin to space, making him the first man to accomplish such a goal. Also, before the US landed Apollo on the moon, the USSR had sent many probes up to the moon along with a probe to Venus and Mars in 1960. In addition to the first man in space, the Soviets also were able to put the first women in space, which was Valentina Tereshkova in 1963. Another accomplishment of the USSR is that they carried out the first space walk in 1965. Obviously all of these major accomplishments for the Soviet space program provided many reason for tension between the US and USSR during the space race and arms race.

Figure 5.2
Example of Ineffective Feedback for Student Writing

Paragraphing Skills: Structure a paragraph to make a point and to have that point contained in a topic sentence.

~~This is why~~ I like dogs better than cats. I think dogs are really playful. They can also be strong to pull you or something. They can come in diferent sizes like a Great Dane or a ~~Wener dog~~ Dachshund. They can also be in diferent colors. Some are just mutts. others are pedigree. Best of all dogs are cute and cuddly. That is why I like dogs a lot better than cats.

Source: *How to Give Effective Feedback* (p. 79), by S. Brookhart, 2008, Alexandria, VA: ASCD. Adapted with permission.

assessment that is specific to criteria and corrective in nature should be common sense, even if it is not common practice. Grant Wiggins (2006) uses a conclusion initially drawn by Richard Light to describe the impact of effective feedback from the students' perspective. He says

> The big point—it comes up over and over again as crucial—is the importance of quick and detailed feedback. Students overwhelmingly report that the single most important ingredient for making a course effective is getting rapid response on assignments and quizzes. An overwhelming majority are convinced that their best learning takes place when they have a chance to submit an early version of their work, get detailed feedback and criticism, and then hand in a final version. (p. 50)

How can high school teachers provide the kind of feedback that students are asking for?

Using Scoring Scales with Students

Well-constructed scoring scales or rubrics provide a way for teachers to give students feedback that tells them what they are learning, how well they are progressing, and what they need to do to get better. When teachers use rubrics as scoring guides, they can explain the levels of performance to students and help them focus on the learning. The rubric depicted in Figure 5.3 is the modified 6+1 Trait Writing model used throughout Littleton High School.

Now that rubrics have become such a part of the education scene, there are many Web sites that teachers can use to construct them. RubiStar is a Web site that has generic rubrics that teachers can use to fit their local learning goals on a variety of topics and skills. These rubrics are available at http://rubistar.4teachers.org. In Figure 5.4, I used RubiStar to construct a rubric based on three traits of the 6+1 Trait Writing model used at Littleton High School.

Of course, the quality of the rubrics used in U.S. high schools today can vary considerably. Teachers must examine scoring scales carefully to be certain that the criteria are focused squarely on the intended learning goal rather than tangential assignment factors, such as project appearance. Figures 5.5 and 5.6 show the distinction between two criteria for a learning goal focused on topography, natural resources, and culture. This first criteria in Figure 5.5 gives students instructions on how to present their projects while the second criteria in Figure 5.6 actually shows students what knowledge they will gain after they complete the assignment.

Teachers can gain a great deal by working in teams to examine rubrics and scoring scales and to ensure that students will receive quality feedback and rigor.

Using a Generic Scoring Scale

Robert Marzano (2006) suggests that teachers can use generic scoring scales across measurement topics in the classroom or classrooms within a school or district. This suggestion is based on research that shows a significant improvement in student achievement when they are given feedback using a framework of tight logic (see Figure 5.7). The logic in this scoring scale begins when the

(text continued on page 72)

Figure 5.3

Writing Power Standards at Littleton High School

Anchor Document for Writing Power Standard						
Score	**Ideas and Content**	**Organization**	**Voice**	**Word Choice**	**Sentence Fluency**	**Conventions**
3–4	• Clear, focused topic • Relevant and accurate supporting details	• Clear introduction, body, and satisfying conclusion • Thoughtful transitions that clearly show how ideas are connected • Sequencing is logical and effective	• Tone furthers purpose and appeals to audience • Appropriately individual and expressive	• Words are specific and accurate • Language and phrasing is natural, effective, and appropriate	• Sentence construction produces natural flow and rhythm	• Grammar and usage are correct and contribute to clarity and style
1–2	• Broad topic • Support is general or insufficient	• Recognizable beginning, middle, and end • Transitions often work well; sometimes connections between ideas are fuzzy • Sequencing is functional	• Tone is appropriate for purpose and audience • Not fully engaged or involved	• Words are adequate and support the meaning • Language is general but functional	• Sentences are constructed correctly	• Grammar and usage mistakes do not impede meaning
0	• Unclear topic • Lacking or irrelevant support	• No apparent organization • Lack of transitions • Sequencing is illogical	• Not concerned with audience or fails to match purpose • Indifferent or inappropriate	• Improper word choice • Usage makes writing difficult to understand • Language is vague or redundant	• Sentences are choppy, incomplete, or unnatural	• Grammar and usage mistakes distract the reader or impede meaning

Figure 5.4

RubiStar Rubric Sample for 6+1 Trait Writing Model

6+1 Trait Writing Model: Demo

Teacher Name: T Westerberg

Student Name: ____________________

CATEGORY	4	3	2	1
Sentence Structure (Sentence Fluency)	All sentences are well-constructed with varied structure.	Most sentences are well-constructed with varied structure.	Most sentences are well-constructed but have a similar structure.	Sentences lack structure and appear incomplete or rambling.
Word Choice	Writer uses vivid words and phrases that linger or draw pictures in the reader's mind, and the choice and placement of the words seem accurate, natural and not forced.	Writer uses vivid words and phrases that linger or draw pictures in the reader's mind, but occasionally the words are used inaccurately or seem overdone.	Writer uses words that communicate clearly, but the writing lacks variety, punch, or flair.	Writer uses a limited vocabulary that does not communicate strongly or capture the reader's interest. Jargon or clichés may be present and detract from the meaning.
Focus on Topic (Content)	There is one clear, well-focused topic. Main idea stands out and is supported by detailed information.	Main idea is clear but the supporting information is general.	Main idea is somewhat clear but there is a need for more supporting information.	The main idea is not clear. There is a seemingly random collection of information.

Source: Rubric made using RubiStar (http://rubistar.4teacher.org)

Figure 5.5

Example of Ineffective Criteria for a Student Project

	What Is the Focus of the Criteria?
4	All sections of the brochure are **complete and handed in on time**, and **optional** sections are included. There are **more than three facts** in each major section. The brochure design is neat, creative, colorful, and typed.
3	All required sections of the brochure are complete and handed in on time. There are at least three facts in each major section. The brochure is neat and easy to read.

Source: D. Pickering, Littleton, CO. Reprinted with permission.

Figure 5.6

Example of Effective Criteria for a Student Project

	What Is the Focus of the Criteria?
4	The student demonstrated an **in-depth understanding** of the interaction of culture, topography, and natural resources. The student discussed the most important interactions in class, and the student also included some interactions that were not obvious and could be easily missed.
3	The student demonstrated a solid, accurate understanding of the interaction of culture, topography, and natural resources. The student showed the most important interactions.

Source: D. Pickering, Littleton, CO. Reprinted with permission.

teacher identifies both the simple and complex knowledge and processes for a particular topic. Next, the teacher lists the simple processes in Level 2 (Score 2.0) and the more complex processes in Level 3 (Score 3.0). After the knowledge and processes have been identified, the teacher can use the scale to give students a score based on their performance. Figure 5.8 shows an example of a scoring scale for a unit on number sense and number systems.

Figure 5.7
Generic Scoring Scale

Score 4.0: **In addition to Score 3.0 performance, in-depth inferences and applications that go beyond what was taught.**
Score 3.5: In addition to Score 3.0 performance, partial success at inferences and applications that go beyond what was taught.
Score 3.0: **No major errors or omissions regarding any of the information and/or processes (simple or complex) that were explicitly taught.**
Score 2.5: No major errors or omissions regarding the simpler details and processes and partial knowledge of the more complex ideas and processes.
Score 2.0: **No major errors or omissions regarding the simpler details and processes but major errors or omissions regarding the more complex ideas and processes.**
Score 1.5: Partial knowledge of the simpler details and processes but major errors or omissions regarding the more complex ideas and processes.
Score 1.0: **With help, a partial understanding of some of the simpler details and processes and some of the more complex ideas and processes.**
Score 0.5: With help, a partial understanding of some of the simpler details and processes but not the more complex ideas and processes.
Score 0.0: **Even with help, no understanding or skill demonstrated.**

Source: *The Art and Science of Teaching* (p. 21), by R. Marzano, 2007, Alexandria, VA: ASCD. Adapted with permission.

Figure 5.8
Generic Scoring Scale for Numbers and Operations

Grade 8		
Score 4.0	**In addition to score 3.0 performance, the student demonstrates in-depth inferences and applications that go beyond what was taught.**	
	Score 3.5	In addition to score 3.0 performance, the student demonstrates in-depth inferences and applications with partial success.
Score 3.0	**While engaged in grade-appropriate tasks, the student demonstrates an understanding of numbers and number systems by . . .** • determining the union and intersection of various sets (*e.g., explaining and exemplifying the union of two sets as the set of elements that are in either set*); • using scientific notation to express large numbers and small numbers between 0 and 1 (*e.g., 0.256 written in scientific notation is* 2.56×10^{-1}); and • distinguishing between subsets of the real number system (*e.g., explaining and exemplifying that a rational number is one that can be written as a simple fraction and providing examples of rational versus irrational numbers*). **The student exhibits no major errors or omissions.**	
	Score 2.5	The student exhibits no major errors or omissions regarding the score 2.0 elements and partial knowledge of the score 3.0 elements.
Score 2.0	**The student exhibits no major errors or omissions regarding the simpler details and processes, such as . . .** • recognizing and recalling specific terminology (*e.g., union, intersection, real number system*); and • recognizing and recalling the accuracy of basic solutions and information, such as . . . ◦ if set A = {1, 3, 5} and set B = {1, 5, 6}, the union of A and B, written $A \cup B$ = {1, 3, 5, 6}; ◦ in scientific notation, numbers are written using powers of 10 (*e.g., 2,000 in scientific notation is* 2×10^3); and ◦ pi is a famous irrational number. **However, the student exhibits major errors or omissions with score 3.0 elements.**	
	Score 1.5	The student demonstrates partial knowledge of the score 2.0 elements but major errors or omissions regarding the score 3.0 elements.
Score 1.0	**With help, the student demonstrates partial understanding of some of the score 2.0 elements and some of the score 3.0 elements.**	
	Score 0.5	With help, the student demonstrates partial understanding of some of the score 2.0 elements but not the score 3.0 elements.
Score 0.0	**Even with help, the student demonstrates no understanding or skill.**	

Source: *Making Standards Useful in the Classroom* (p. 117), by R. Marzano & M. Haystead, 2008, Alexandria, VA: ASCD. Adapted with permission.

Whether teachers use the generic format suggested by Marzano or other formats that differ across disciplines and topics, scoring scales and rubrics help students see what good work looks like and how to get better next time. These factors are critical features of effective feedback.

Effectively Using Grading

The grades that students receive on their transcripts at the end of a grading period are summative, not formative, assessments. Although these grades serve accountability and reporting purposes rather than the instructional purposes advocated for in this chapter, final grades are part of the feedback students receive and thus merit more analysis.

Grading in the vast majority of high schools in this country is messy and unfair to kids. That is a strong statement, but I have received a surprising degree of agreement from high school teachers and administrators once the current realities about grades are exposed. What are those realities?

Grades should reflect a student's demonstrated mastery of identified course learning goals. Instead, grades in many high schools often reflect what I refer to as the Prego approach to grading. My description of current grading practices is an offshoot of a Prego spaghetti sauce commercial from a couple of decades ago. In the commercial, a stereotypical Italian woman goes to her son and daughter-in-law's house for a spaghetti dinner. The young couple keeps the mother in the living room while they prepare the meal in the kitchen because they do not want her to know that they are using a sauce from the store rather than making it from scratch. She becomes suspicious, bursts into the kitchen, and to her horror, finds the Prego spaghetti sauce. When she exclaims "What about the oregano?" her son says, "Ma, it's in there." "What about the celery?" "Ma, it's in there." "What about the fresh basil?" "Ma, it's in there."

Far too many high schools are using the Prego approach to grading. Teachers are including everything in a student's grade from academic achievement to affective behaviors to a student's disposition. If teachers need to show students' demonstrated mastery of course learning goals in their grades? Yes, that's in there. Extra credit? Yes, that's in there. Points off for tardies and absences? That's in there. Points for good behavior? That's in there, too. When teachers use a Prego approach to evaluate students, the grades are almost meaningless.

The Absence of Effective Standards for Grading

I found interesting an article in the *Washington Post* (Mathews, 2007) in which parents in Fairfax County, Virginia, were complaining that students needed a 94 percent to get an *A* in their school whereas across the river in Montgomery County, Maryland, students could receive an *A* for earning marks of 90 and above. "There are no effective standards," said Robert Hartranft, a retired nuclear engineer from Simsbury, Maryland, who was scrutinizing the issue. "Local grades and local GPAs are a crazy quilt of numerical values and systems" (p. A01).

You don't have to be a rocket scientist or a nuclear engineer to figure this one out. What I find most interesting, however, is that the concerned parties are not addressing the fundamental issue. The assumption in the argument is that if the two counties used the same grading scale, then grading for thousands of students in both counties would be consistent and fair. From our earlier discussion in Chapter 3, we know that a 90 isn't the same between teachers in the same school, let alone across schools and districts. Unless teachers are regularly talking about what the major learning goals are, explicitly defining what it looks like when students get it right, and using common scoring scales or rubrics, a common grading scale is nothing more than subjectivity masquerading as objectivity.

In another news story, parents asked questions about grading systems in Pittsburgh area schools. In that district, only one in five students received a GPA of 4.6 or higher, while students with a GPA of 3.3 or lower were ranked in the bottom half of their class. The title of that article is quite telling of what is happening to grading systems in American high schools: "In high schools, a 'B' is new 'C': Higher grades not matched by higher test scores" (Chute, 2007).

In *The Learning Leader*, Doug Reeves (2006) draws on comparisons between achievement as measured by state exams and grade point averages to support the contention that there are no effective standards in the grading systems in most high school classrooms in this country. In one comparison, Reeves examines the average grade point averages of high-achieving and low-achieving students. They are essentially the same. In another comparison, Reeves looks at the percent of students receiving *D*s and *F*s and the percent of students receiving *A*s, *B*s, and *C*s who fail state high school math and language arts exams. Again, there are no significant differences in the failure rates of the two groups.

We completed a similar analysis several years ago at Littleton High School. In our case we plotted the relationship between students' performance on state reading, writing, and mathematics tests with their grades in their language arts and math classes. We found no correlation. Students with low achievement scores were no more or no less likely to earn high grades in the corresponding classes than were students who scored proficient or advanced on the state tests. Such an analysis would be of value in every school.

What can we conclude from the analyses conducted by Reeves and the staff at Littleton High School? Are state exams seriously flawed? Are classroom instruction and assessment not truly standards based? Assuming that we have identified learning course goals appropriately, are classroom grades not an accurate reflection of these goals? Some measure of each of these conjectures may be in effect, but the last two explanations are definitely part of the problem, given the prevalence of several questionable grading practices in our high schools.

Examining Highly Questionable Grading Practices

My style as a principal was to issue dictates sparingly. In 20 years as principal at Littleton High school, I probably said, "Read my lips" only a half dozen times. You do not get to stay at one school for 20 years if you are always issuing unilateral orders. Instead, my style was to challenge the staff with data, professional opinion, research, and even moral imperatives, and then I would let the staff ruminate on the issue awhile. Occasionally, a critical mass of staff members would decide to act after a time, and, in a few cases, behaviors actually changed.

The latter strategy was how I approached the topic of grading practices with the faculty in the fall of 2004. I challenged the faculty by declaring, with some passion, that the practices we were using were *highly* questionable and should be discontinued. I did not say that they had to be discontinued, but rather that they should be stopped. The teachers were hot. Hands were in the air, people followed me out of the room with questions and counterarguments, and discussions continued into the parking lot. I loved it. High school teachers feel very strongly about their grading practices. To question how they grade is to question who they are and their reasons for being in the profession. Here are the challenges that got them so stirred up.

The Practice of Giving Students Zeroes

Giving students zeroes for work not turned in is not good practice on several fronts. First, putting zeroes in the grade book for missing assignments does not make sense mathematically, especially if they are used in conjunction with the time-honored 100-point system. For example, if we use a grading scale wherein a student receives a *D* for earning 60–70 percent, a *C* for earning 70–80 percent, a *B* for earning 80–90, and an *A* for earning 90–100 percent, the interval between a zero and a low *D* is 60 points. On the other hand, the interval between a *D* and a *C* or between any other two letter grades is only 10 points. The effect of this interval difference places a greater weight on the zero than any other grade the student earns. If Johnny scores a perfect 100 on the next assignment of equal importance, he still has an *F* (50%) in the class. Johnny may not do well in math, but he can figure out that it will take many top grades to balance out one zero.

The second reason that giving zeroes is not sound practice is because it does not encourage students to keep trying. The mathematical impact of a couple of zeroes early in the semester can lead students to feel hopeless and to abandon their efforts, which only compounds the problem. As a principal, I witnessed teachers sending students to the guidance office to drop a class at the end of the quarter and telling them they had no chance of passing. It's little wonder that some students mentally check out, or worse, engage in disruptive behaviors after the first few weeks of the semester.

A third reason to question the practice of giving zeroes is that it suggests that the student knows absolutely nothing about the topic at hand. Is that typically the case? Given that you are a good teacher, if a student attends your class just three days a week with minimal engagement and no homework completed, is it possible, under your tutelage, that he or she has learned absolutely nothing? Not in my class. We are seeking a system of grading that accurately reflects what students know and can do based on established learning goals.

Finally, what message do we want to send to students regarding the completion of assigned work? Is it optional? Did the teacher assign some "junk homework" or busy work that really does not need to be completed? Or, is every assignment designed to move students closer to mastery of an important learning goal? Putting a zero in the grade book and moving on suggests that the assignment was not very important in the first place. In high schools where the culture reflects a we-expect-success attitude, teachers do not let students off the hook with incomplete or substandard work. Instead, they convey the message that every assignment, project, quiz, and test is important and *must* be completed.

I am often confronted with the so-called "real world" argument for awarding zeroes for missing assignments. My opponents have argued, "In the real world, there are consequences for not getting your work done or on time. Your employer is not going to say, 'It's okay that you didn't do anything today. Try to get something done tomorrow.' You do that, and you'll get fired."

Well, which "real world" is that? During my career as a principal, I found that the teachers who were the most inflexible regarding missing or late work for their students were also the teachers who missed every deadline for turning in their grades. Yet, none of them was fired, lost pay, or was even reprimanded. We simply implored them to get their grades in as soon as possible. We could all come up with examples of what happens when you do not get a second chance to act responsibly. Drive drunk even once and it could cost you your license or even your life. But, in my own experience, both personal and professional, I have a record of receiving second, third, and sometimes tenth chances. It is seldom that I have been nailed for blowing an assignment or expectation the first time around. It seems to me that real life is a mixed bag of second chances and eventual consequences. Perhaps school life should more accurately replicate this reality.

Some of the alternatives to giving students zeroes for missing work are controversial. One solution to the problem is to move from a 100-point scale that can vary from 10 to 60 points to a scale with consistent single-point intervals. For example, let's say that a teacher decides to use the following grading scale: A = 5 points, B = 4 points, C = 3 points, D = 2 points, and F = 1 point. If a student earns a zero for incomplete work, his grade is not disproportionately weighed by zeroes when the teacher averages his final composite grade. (Averaging is also a questionable grading practice and will be analyzed further on pp. 81–82.)

Another alternative that many schools and districts have adopted is to avoid the discomfort associated with changing the traditional grading system. By maintaining the traditional 100-point system, teachers can give students a 50 for missing assignments instead of a zero. This solution addresses the problem of unequal grading intervals; however, many teachers are uncomfortable with giving students 50 points for doing nothing.

In 2007, the Dallas ISD board of trustees reaffirmed a policy that prevented teachers from giving students anything lower than a 50 during any one grading period. During the 2008–09 school year, the board enforced a stricter policy that prohibited teachers from assigning any penalty for late or missing work. The response from teachers was swift and almost universally negative (Fischer, 2008). Similarly, officials in the Pittsburgh Public Schools received pushback over their renewed efforts to enforce a district policy that set 50 percent as the minimum score a student can receive on any assignment (Smydo, 2008).

Philosophically, I am aligned with school leaders who simply will not settle for zeroes or missing assignments. Glenpool Middle School in Oklahoma adopted a program called Zeroes Aren't Permitted (ZAP). Students at Glenpool who fail to turn in homework must make up their missed work during lunch periods, after school, or other noninstructional time (Vance, 2008). Ben Davis High School in Indianapolis gives students an opportunity to complete missing assignments by using amnesty days. This policy allows students who are failing a course by just a few percentage points to complete missing assignments or demonstrate proficiency during the first weeks of the next semester. Failure rates at the school have been reduced significantly (Nagel, 2008). During my days in school, I have memories of teachers who would not tolerate substandard or missing work. Those teachers hounded me until the work was done, and they often combined forces with my athletic coaches and threatened to involve my parents. The message from these and other likeminded teachers and schools was clear: "What we are doing here is important, you can do it, and we're not going to give up on you."

Requiring students to repeat an entire course because of a few missing assignments is, at best, a questionable use of student time and school resources. Designing ways for high school students to complete missing work rather than repeat an entire course makes both pedagogical and economic sense.

The Practice of Combining Academic Performance with Citizenship and Work Habits

Giving zeroes for incomplete or missing work is actually a subordinate category of a larger highly questionable practice—combining academic performance with citizenship and work habits or life skills into a single grade.

Consider the case of two students enrolled in the same chemistry class. Gayle is a chemistry whiz. She gets *A*s on most major tests and projects, but she does not bother to turn in homework, is often late for class, and was even found guilty of plagiarism on a research paper. Gayle knows her chemistry, but her work habits and ethics are questionable. She earned a combination of high grades and zeroes and has a *C* average for the semester.

For Brian, chemistry does not come as easily. He gets *D*s on most major assessments for chemistry content and skills, but Brian is a great kid. He turns in every assignment (although his work is usually wrong), has perfect attendance, is always on time for class, works well with others, and is as honest as the day is long. Brian is the student whom teachers hire as a babysitter for their own children because of his responsibility and dependability. Brian has low test scores and high grades for homework completion, attendance, and class participation, and he also ends up with a *C* average for the semester.

Gayle and Brian are nothing alike, yet they are both headed off to college or work with *C*s in chemistry on their transcripts. Gayle knows chemistry, but buyers had best beware of her work habits and character. Brian is a great kid. Potential employers should hire him; however, they shouldn't put him to work in a pharmacy.

At Sacramento New Technology High School, students are given separate grades for mastery of course content and for learning outcomes such as collaborating with peers (Gewertz, 2007). At Heritage High School in Colorado, social studies teacher Tony Winger gives students in his economics classes separate grades for academic content (e.g., economic ways of thinking, microeconomics, and macroeconomics), communication and thinking skills (e.g., reading, writing, vocabulary skills, and application of economic concepts), and nonacademic factors (e.g., responsibility and investment). Because his school requires a single course grade at the end of each semester, Winger combines his students' grades in each area to arrive at a final grade. Students and parents can easily identify specific strengths and weaknesses in each area.

Mike Montgomery, a former high school teacher at Littleton High School in Colorado, used a similar approach for separating academic and nonacademic performance in his chemistry classes. He identified what he called product (i.e., Colorado chemistry standards), process (i.e., building reading and writing standards), and progress (i.e., investment, contribution, work completion) criteria. Again, students received separate marks that were combined to form a single course grade for the semester. This practice works against the intent of reporting on academic and nonacademic performance separately, but it goes beyond the limitations of traditional grading and reporting systems. These are less than perfect examples, but they represent significant steps forward.

As principal at Littleton High School, I advocated for teachers to give students two grades on their report cards and transcripts in every course. One grade represented students' demonstrated mastery of academic content and skills, and the other grade reflected their behaviors as identified under the power standards for citizenship and work. Based on local community values, the teachers still needed to decide which grade or combination of grades to use for calculating GPAs and class rank. But, at the very least, students would have two separate grades for their performance. How would colleges and employers use this additional information? I don't know, but at some point that becomes their problem. The school would have done its part to clearly and accurately report a student's academic and nonacademic performance.

The Practice of Giving Extra Credit

Awarding extra credit is inconsistent with standards-based grading. By definition, this work is *extra* or outside the identified guaranteed curriculum. How can we justify allowing students to substitute something extra for essential knowledge and skills? For example, how can we allow students to bring in food for a canned food drive in lieu of successfully completing a required essay? If teaching students the importance of lending a helping hand to fellow human beings is a learning goal in the school community, then school leaders should identify this goal accordingly. However, bringing in food for the food drive should not be an extra learning goal for students. Teachers should not mix points for extra credit with points for demonstrated research and writing skills.

I want to be certain to make a distinction between what I am referring to here as extra credit, which I do not support, and the practice of allowing students multiple opportunities to demonstrate mastery of course learning goals. Requiring students to rewrite a lab report, take another version of the test, or repeat a required dance routine following feedback from the teacher is the aim of formative assessment.

The Practice of Averaging

If the aim of formative assessment is to assist students in reaching a learning goal, and if the aim of the grading system used in a school is to accurately report what students know and can do, then the practice of averaging makes no sense. Let's examine another hypothetical example.

Suppose a student began a unit of instruction on a particular learning goal with *D*s (or 1s on a scoring rubric) on the first two assessments. Let's further assume that the student got his act together and earned *B*s (or 3s) on the next two assessments. The reasons for his improved performance are varied. He could have become concerned about his grades and started working harder, his parents could have taken away the car keys, he could have received help from a tutor, he could have responded to the adjustments his teacher made in instruction, or any number of other factors that could affect his performance. Assuming that the four assessments are of equal weight, what grade will this student receive for this unit of instruction in the vast majority of high school classrooms in the country? You guessed it, a *C*. A *C* is one grade this student never received. The grade that best reflects what this student knows or can do is a *B*.

Averaging is a highly questionable practice because it treats all assessment scores as equal values and builds on the assumption that students haven't learned anything as a result of instruction. When teachers use averaging, the scores that a student received at the beginning of instruction carry the same weight as scores earned later in the instructional progression. One alternative to averaging involves looking at trend scores over time to predict a student's true score on a learning goal or measurement topic at the end of instruction.

Challenging the Point System

High school teachers defend the traditional 100-point system with a fervor that suggests divine intervention. The following case from my years at Littleton High School illustrates the point.

A parent called me in the fall and asked me to look into the grade his daughter received in a particular class during the previous spring semester. The grades for the spring semester didn't go out until the teacher had already left for summer break, and this parent contacted me because the teacher had left the building (in good standing) and was now employed elsewhere.

His daughter had a mid to high *C* going into the final exam and received an *A* on the final. She was certain she would get a *B* in the class, but she received a *C* instead. I contacted the teacher and learned that with her grade for the final exam, this student ended the semester with 79.4 percent. In this teacher's class, students had to have an 80 to get a *B*, but the teacher would round up to an 80 percent if students received 79.5 percent and above. This student missed earning a *B* by .1 of one percent out of hundreds of points for that semester. I would have given that student a *B* in a heartbeat.

Let me skip to the end of the story and come back to the middle. That student still has a *C* on her transcript for that course. In 26 years as a principal, I never changed a grade. This teacher had been with her students every day, therefore, she was in the best position to make a judgment about any particular student's performance. In a meeting with the parent and me, the teacher added up the student's points, divided that number by the total, and then, with calculator screen pointed toward the parent, said, "See, 79.4 percent." But, when she added, "And there is nothing I can do about it," I found myself rising out of my chair. The teacher might as well have said, "God speaks to me through the medium of the calculator. I am just his messenger." Amazingly, the parent bought it, agreeing with the infallibility of the 100-point system and the judgment of the calculator.

When the parent left, I asked the teacher, "Are you nuts? Do you mean to tell me that there is no error in assessment? Even the most scientifically designed studies include a margin of error. Do you really believe that there is a significant difference in learning between a 79.4 and a 79.5 or for that matter between a 79.4 and an 81.2?" The teacher responded with, "Well, the calculator..." I interrupted her and I said, "Don't tell me what the calculator says. I want to know what grade you think best represents the student's mastery of important course content and skills."

The point of this story is that teachers shouldn't just arbitrarily assign student grades. Ultimately, grades are just judgments, not true scores, and teachers need to be able to support their judgments. Many teachers place too much confidence in the traditional 100-point grading system, which has been proven to be seriously flawed. Is there an alternative?

Using Standards-Based Grading

In *Classroom Assessment and Grading That Work,* Robert Marzano (2006) details a system of standards-based grading based on the generic rubric discussed earlier in this chapter (see p. 72). In Marzano's grading system, he proposes that teachers use frequent formative assessments, unpack state standards to form a limited number of unique elements of knowledge and skills called measurement topics, look at trend scores using a mathematic model known as the power law, and move away from using averaging within measurement topics. He also recommends that teachers identify and evaluate academic and nonacademic measurement topics using the same generic rubric format and gather additional assessment data from students for missing assignments instead of giving them zeros. Finally, he proposes that teachers can use the rubric scores for course measurement topics and combine and convert them to traditional grades to comply with district or state grade-reporting requirements.

My colleague, Mary McDonough, has developed a classification graphic organizer to illustrate the difference between traditional and standards-based grading systems (see Figure 5.9).

The relevant questions for high school educators are, "Does our grading system accurately reflect mastery of identified learning goals?" and "Is our grading system fair to students?"

There is a better mousetrap out there, albeit it is one that calls for considerable rethinking of the values and beliefs undergirding classroom assessment and grading in most U.S. high schools. If I were to become a high school principal again (and I'm not), I would give serious consideration to using standards-based grading as my primary vehicle of school improvement. A thorough examination of most grading practices would expose so many curricular, instructional, and assessment elephants in the room.

You can't have standards-based grading without clear standards or learning goals. When teachers use formative assessment, it is assumed that they understand what good work looks like for individual learning goals and provide frequent corrective feedback to students. When grading practices are honestly and carefully examined, teachers and administrators can have open conversations about topics such as trend scores, averaging, and missing work, and they can take a systemic look at high school norms, policies, and practices. Classroom assessment and grading can be a high-leverage school improvement tool in a high school with the capacity to manage it. Not every school presently has the capacity to look at classroom assessment and grading practices, but that is not an excuse for inaction. Individual schools and teachers can work on pieces of this elephant and make small, significant improvements in assessment practices. In many cases there is not one right answer, but pretending that these issues do not exist and remaining silent is clearly the wrong thing to do.

Figure 5.9
Traditional and Standards–Based Grading

Standards for Record Keeping, Designing and Scoring Tests, and Determining Final Grades

Traditional System	**Standards-Based System**
1. Grades are based on potluck content design and scoring	1. Rubrics are designed and scored by identifying content
2. Assessments are used for grading	2. Grades are awarded by using standards and topics
3. Grades are awarded by comparing students with each other	3. Grading accounts for progress toward standards
4. Grades include criteria such as effort, timeliness, etc.	4. Grading separates academic and nonacademic standards
5. Grades are awarded by averaging scores	5. Grading allows for student progress according to Power Law
6. Grades on report cards include general content (e.g., ELA writing)	6. Graded content is specifically labeled and aligned with standards
7. Teachers keep records in handwritten grade book	7. Teachers use a computer to record grades

Source: M. McDonough, Centerville, MA. Reprinted with permission.

Giving students effective feedback using frequent formative assessment that are clearly focused on learning goals is a powerful instructional force. As Grant Wiggins (2006) puts it, "The more you teach without finding out who understands the information and who doesn't, [it's more] likely that only already-proficient students will succeed" (p. 50). Properly designed scoring scales or rubrics serve to structure and guide feedback. Current classroom assessment and grading practices in most high school classrooms are based on unexamined assumptions and questionable practices that are inconsistent with formative assessment, continuous progress, and standards-based instruction. Fortunately, models are now available that bridge the gaps between best practices and common practices.

6

Strategy 4: Tracking Student Progress

In the high school we have been building thus far in this book, a high school that is making the jump from being good to becoming great, teachers agree on clear, course-level learning goals, communicate these goals to students, and deliver well-designed units of instruction. They work in course-level or department teams to collaboratively develop rubrics or scoring scales detailing targeted levels of performance for course learning goals. These teachers also use common assessments or items drawn from an assessment bank to provide students with frequent corrective feedback at appropriate points in the learning progression. By this point, our school has already become a high-performing organization. The next step in this process is to design opportunities for students, teachers, teams of teachers, and, perhaps even schools and districts, to track student progress.

Displaying Students' Results Graphically

For more than a decade, formative assessment pioneer Rick Stiggins has been an advocate for student involvement in record keeping as both a powerful trigger for productive emotions and as a research-based strategy for increasing student achievement ("Using asssessment," 1997). It is motivating for students to see that they are making progress toward an important learning goal, even if they are not yet performing at the highest level as identified by a rubric.

Stiggins's support for student record keeping by using a variety of different formats, such as graphically displaying results from formative assessments, is well documented by research. Perhaps the most often cited research on the impact of graphically displaying student results is the 1986 study by Fuchs and Fuchs. In their meta-analysis of 89 studies, the Fuchs found an average

26 percentile point gain in student achievement when students were asked to graphically track their progress on learning goals. Students can easily be taught to construct simple line or bar graphs, such as the graph displayed in Figure 6.1, to track their progress on an identified learning goal.

Figure 6.1
Tracking Student Learning with Bar Graphs

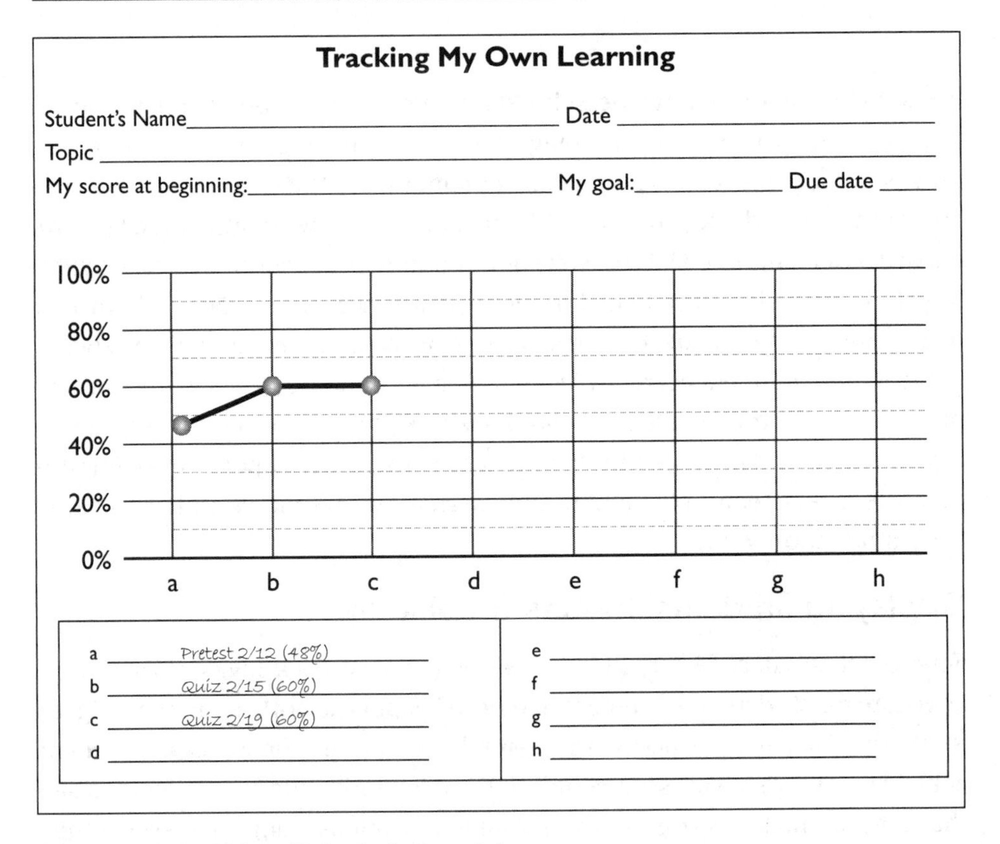

Source: D. Pickering, Littleton, CO. Reprinted with permission.

By combining the focus on effort-based learning discussed in Chapter 1 with tracking student progress, teachers can show students how to graphically display both their academic progress and the effort they put forth during a unit of instruction. Figure 6.2 shows an example of a rubric that students can use to assess their efforts.

Figure 6.2
Tracking Student Learning with Effort Rubrics

CATEGORY	4 – Proficient	3 – Meets Standard	2 – Emerging	1 – Not Acceptable
Class Notes	I take neat notes, keep them neatly organized in a binder, and refer to them every day when doing class work and homework.	I take neat notes, keep them neatly organized in a binder, and usually refer to them often when doing class work and homework.	I take notes, but they are messy or unorganized; I use them occasionally when doing class work and homework.	I often do not take notes or do not keep notes; I almost never refer to notes when doing class work and homework.
Attention	I pay attention in class, listen carefully to the teacher's questions, and focus on the class work at least 95% of the time.	I pay attention in class, listen to the teacher's questions, and focus on the class work 80–95% of the time.	I pay attention in class most of the time. If I am called on, I often know the question the teacher is asking. I focus on the class work 70–80% of the time.	I am off task more than 70% of the time, not listening to instruction. If I am called on, I usually don't know the question, and I don't focus on the class work.
Participation	I ask at least 2 questions a day and volunteer at least 2 answers a day when offered the opportunity, even if I'm not sure my answers are right.	I ask 1 question per day and volunteer 1 answer per day when offered the opportunity, but usually only when I'm certain of being right.	I ask 1– 4 questions per week and offer to answer questions 1–4 times per week, but only when I'm certain of being right.	I rarely ask questions or volunteer answers.
Homework	I attempt all problems on every homework assignment, even if I think some of my answers might be incorrect. I refer to class notes while doing homework	I attempt all problems on homework 4 nights per week, even if I think some of my answers might be incorrect. I usually refer to class notes while doing homework.	I attempt most homework problems but not those that seem difficult or confusing. I miss several homework assignments each week and occasionally use notes often when doing homework.	I miss many homework assignments and skip many answers, particularly those problems that appear long or difficult. I almost never refer to class notes when doing homework.
Studying	I begin studying for a test as soon as it is announced. I study class notes for at least 10 minutes per day every day until the test, and attempt 2–3 practice problems.	I begin studying for a test 3–5 days before the test. I study class notes for 5–10 minutes per day every day until the test, and attempt 1–2 practice problems.	I begin studying for a test 2 days before the test. I study class notes for 5–10 minutes each day, and do not attempt practice problems.	I study for the test the night before only. I study class notes sometimes and do not attempt practice problems.

Source: *Using Technology with Classroom Instruction That Works* (p. 157), by H. Pitler, E.R. Hubbell, M. Kuhn, & K. Malenoski, 2007, Alexandria, VA: ASCD. Adapted with permission.

When students use the rubric shown in Figure 6.2 and a scoring scale designed for the learning goal under study, a student's graph might look similar to the one displayed in Figure 6.3.

Figure 6.3
Tracking Student Progress with a Graph

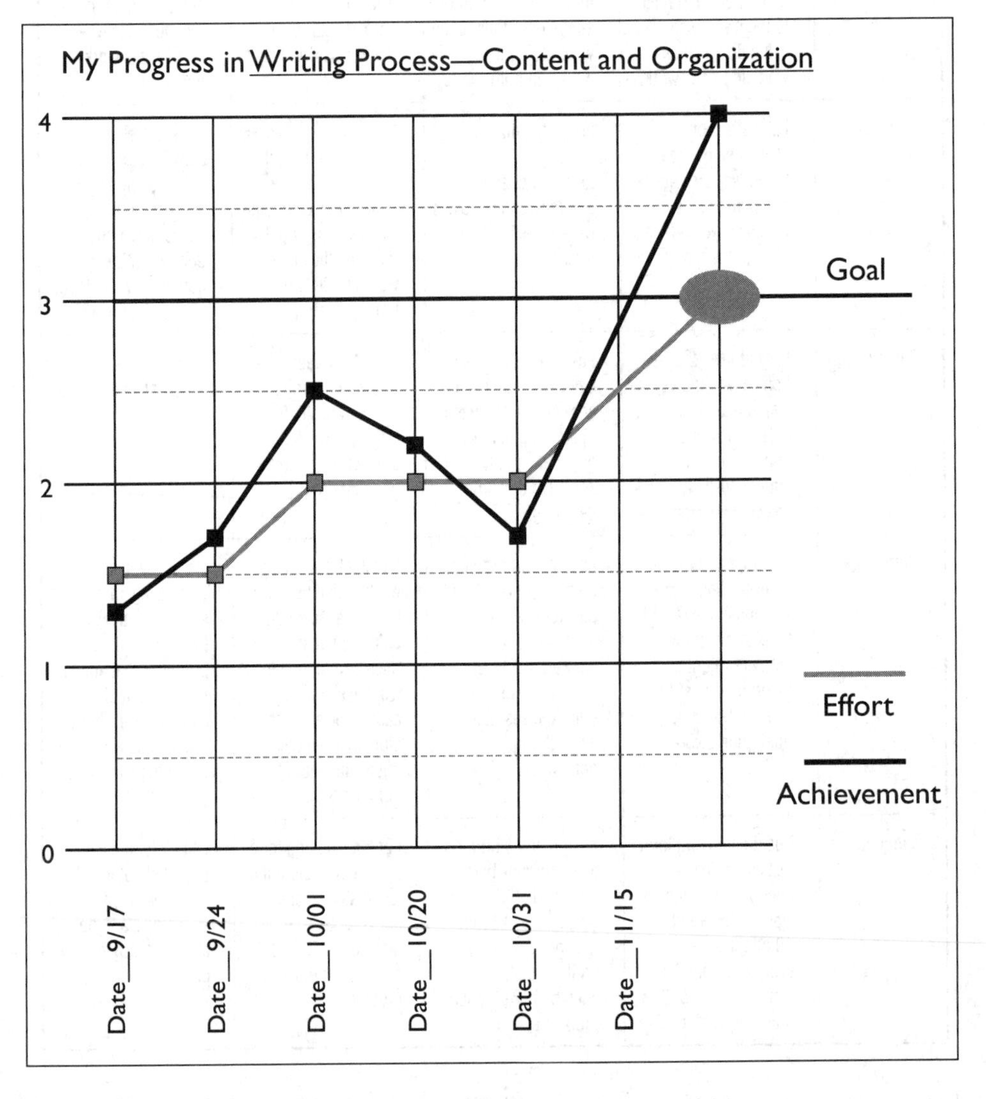

Source: D. Pickering, Littleton, CO. Reprinted with permission.

By graphically displaying effort and achievement together, students not only see that they are making progress toward the learning goal, but also that there is a positive relationship between effort and achievement. Of course, when students extend their effort, this does not always result in higher achievement. Sometimes students work hard and still score low because of any number of intervening variables. There are also times when they get lucky and score well despite not being fully prepared. But, over the long haul, the more effort students put into an initiative, the better their results, and that is a lesson we want students to internalize.

Using Tracking for Teachers and Teacher Teams

Graphically displaying assessment results for a class or for an entire grade on specific learning goals can aid teachers in analyzing their instructional effectiveness and celebrating success. Figures 6.4 and 6.5 display the results of an individual teacher's and a group of teachers' efforts to graphically display aggregate student progress on a writing goal.

Tracking results from formative assessments for specific learning goals provides individual teachers with ongoing information on how the class is progressing overall and the effectiveness of the instructional strategies employed. For example, if students are not writing stronger persuasive essays after written feedback on three consecutive literature-based essay assignments, alternative approaches should be considered. Perhaps peer editing or individual student conferences with the teacher will produce positive results. Conversely, if the teacher observes improved performance for the whole class after a couple of assignments, he or she is justified in continuing the instructional strategies currently used. Formative assessment results for some students may indicate a need for alternative strategies.

Teachers in high-performing high schools are not working in isolation. Instead, they meet regularly with colleagues in professional learning communities or in other structured collaborative arrangements to analyze student performance data and samples of students' work and discuss instructional strategies that the data indicate are producing positive results. For example, all English 10 teachers meet twice a month to discuss each teacher's class data on persuasive writing. During these meetings they identify strategies that are producing desired results and make suggestions for adjusting instruction based on performance data. Without this kind of data, adjustments for each teacher's instruction are either based on an individual teacher's hunches or not made at all.

Figure 6.4
Tracking Individual Teachers with Learning Goals and Graphs

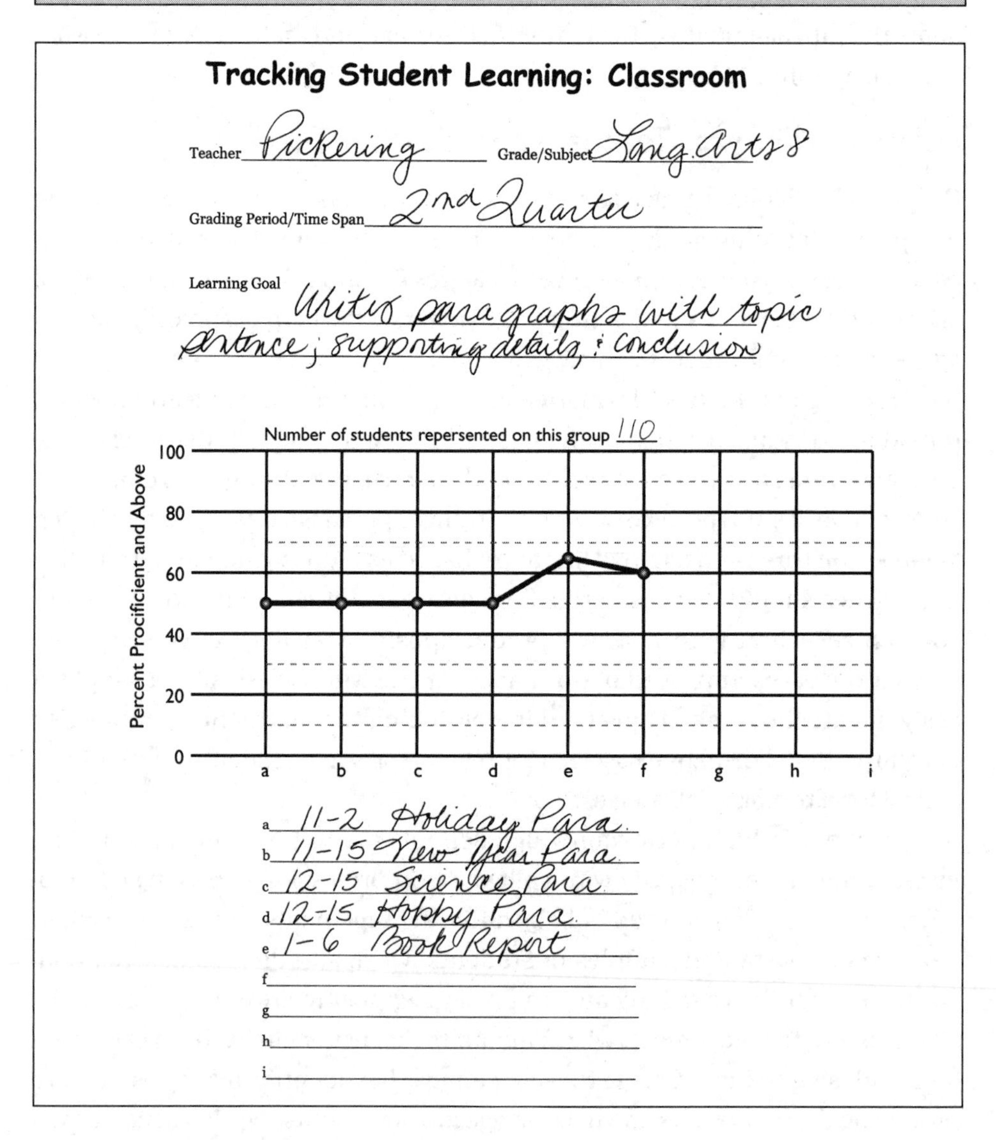

Source: D. Pickering, Littleton, CO. Reprinted with permission.

Figure 6.5
Tracking Teacher Teams with Learning Goals and Graphs

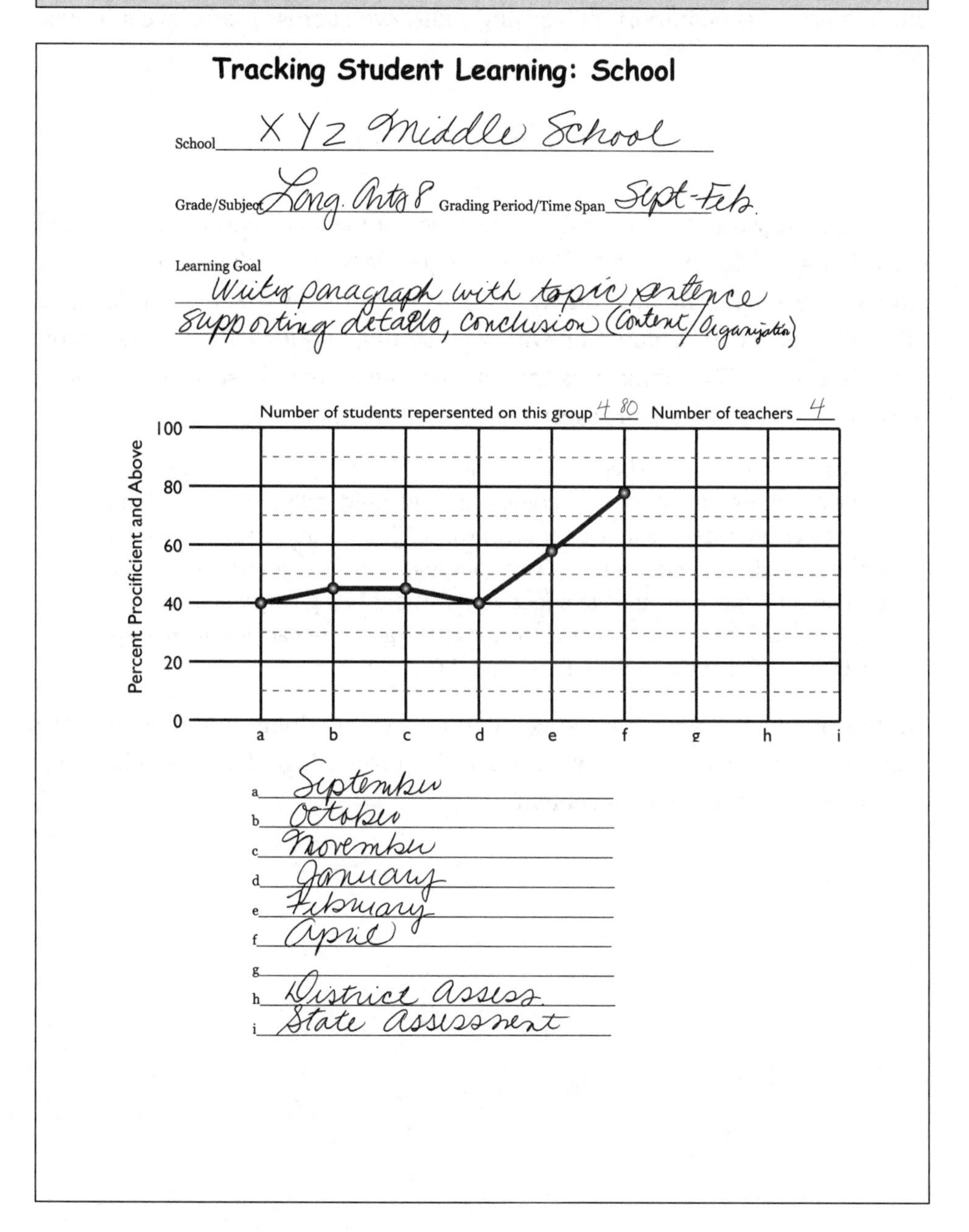

Tracking Student Learning: School

School XYZ Middle School

Grade/Subject Lang. Arts 8 Grading Period/Time Span Sept-Feb.

Learning Goal
Write paragraph with topic sentence supporting details, conclusion (Content/Organization)

Number of students repersented on this group 480 Number of teachers 4

a September
b October
c November
d January
e February
f April
g
h District Assess.
i State Assessment

Source: D. Pickering, Littleton, CO. Reprinted with permission.

This same type of graph could be used to aggregate data at the district level as well. Administrators in the Baltimore County school system are testing a computerized system that allows teachers and parents to systematically track student progress on important learning goals, even across grade levels (Davis, 2007).

Graphically tracking student progress on course-level learning goals at the individual student, class, school, and district levels is a powerful learning tool for students, teachers, and administrators. This is a strategy that high-performing high schools use in conjunction with goal setting and formative assessment. Rick Stiggins (2007) summarizes the relationship among these strategies with the following description of assessment for learning. He says

> Assessment for learning begins when teachers share improvement targets with students, presenting those expectations in student-friendly language accompanied by examples of exemplary student work. Then, frequent self-assessments provide students (and teachers) with continual access to descriptive feedback in amounts they can manage effectively without being overwhelmed. Thus, students can chart their trajectory toward the transparent achievement targets their teachers have established. (pp. 22–23)

When students know what is expected, how they are doing, and how they are progressing, these are effective strategies for promoting effort-based learning and increasing student achievement.

7

Strategy 5: Providing Timely Intervention for Struggling Students

Many good high schools boast of having high academic standards; however, great high schools have high standards and an uncommonly high percentage of rather "common" students who meet these standards. Teachers, administrators, and other personnel in high-performing high schools understand motivation theory and the strategies and conditions that promote student engagement, as well as the importance of using engagement to boost students' academic success.

High schools that move from good to great do so by complementing a we-expect-success attitude with practices, structures, and programs that help students meet high academic expectations. The question we turn to now is, "How can we support students who need extra time and help to succeed in challenging programs of study?"

Using Self-System Thinking and Student Engagement

How a student feels about the content or skills to be learned and his or her relationship with the material will greatly affect how invested he or she will be. Investment or engagement is crucial to a student's success in a rigorous academic program. One of the levels of mental processing identified by Marzano and Kendall (2008) in their New Taxonomy of Educational Objectives is the Self-System. According to Marzano and Kendall, the Self-System determines the extent to which an individual will engage in a task and how much energy the individual will invest in learning. The self-system consists of four types of thinking that affect student engagement: importance, efficacy, emotional response, and motivation.

Importance is defined as the extent to which an individual considers the knowledge as either satisfying a basic need or instrumental in accomplishing a personal goal. You can recall the "What we're doing here is important" message of the we-expect-success attitude presented in Chapter 2. The connection between the importance or relevance and student engagement is well established in school improvement literature (DuFour, Eaker, & DuFour, 2005; Marzano & Kendall, 2008; National Association of Secondary School Principals, 2004). Few leaders in high school education today have escaped the familiar battle cry of high school reform: rigor, relevance, and relationships!

Efficacy is about the extent to which a learner believes he or she has what it takes (i.e., ability, resources, and necessary support) to accomplish the task at hand. My own motivation to work on this book increased as I became convinced about midway through the process that "Hey, I can do this!" Efficacy relates with a "You can do it" outlook and the effort-based learning component of a we-expect-success attitude. In a recent study on ways to get more girls to pursue careers in math and science conducted by vocational psychologists at the University of Wisconsin-Milwaukee, Nadya Fouad, a distinguished professor, concluded, "The relationship between confidence and interest is close. If they feel they can do it, it feeds their interest" ("Tracking the reasons," 2008).

A student's belief that he or she has the resources and support necessary to learn what is expected is also a part of efficacy, and as such, is the subject of this chapter on timely intervention.

Emotions play a big role in our motivation to engage. How we feel about the content or skills to be learned based on past experiences with that knowledge constitutes our emotional response to knowledge. If I have always hated working with fractions, due in large part to my lack of success in that arena in the past, I am unlikely to invest much energy in the topic in the future. Emotional response is affected by relationships with teachers and is therefore encompassed in the rigor, relevance, relationships mantra. An individual's overall motivation to engage in a particular learning task is a function of his or her perception of the importance, efficacy, and emotional response relative to a particular knowledge component or learning task.

Marzano and Kendall (2008) posit that a student's high motivation to learn a particular knowledge component exists under the following conditions:

- The individual perceives the knowledge component as important.
- The individual believes that he or she has the necessary ability, power, or resources to learn or increase competence relative to the knowledge component.
- The individual has a positive emotional response to the knowledge component (or both 2 and 3). (p. 24)

Low motivation to learn is likely to occur when the converse conditions are present.

Ronald Ferguson of Harvard labels the kind of instructional design that combines clear learning goals with attention to self-efficacy as "high perfectionism and high help" (Viadero, 2008, p. 14). Geoffrey Cohen of the University of Colorado agrees with Ferguson, recommending that "in offering students critical feedback, teachers [should] convey the idea that the criticism reflects a high standard, and that they believe in the student's ability to reach that standard" (Viadero, 2008, p. 14). Similarly, Wiggins and McTighe (2007) identify the following four variables that promote student engagement:

- The learner clearly sees the learning goals and understands what is expected.
- The content is seen as relevant and useful to learn.
- The learner perceives that he or she is capable of succeeding at the learning tasks.
- The learner feels accepted and supported by the teacher. (p. 141)

Although the conditions or variables identified by these researchers are to some extent interdependent, this chapter deals primarily with Marzano and Kendall's second condition: To what extent do our high schools provide the resources and support that students need to fully engage in learning and maximize academic success in rigorous programs of study?

Implementing Practices, Structures, and Programs That Support Student Success

High-performing high schools have context-specific practices, structures, and programs in place that not only allow for but actually require timely intervention when the results of early formative assessments indicate that students have not grasped critical components of a knowledge progression. Probably the best way to illustrate this point is through examples of what successful districts and schools are doing to intervene and support their students.

The Long Beach Unified School District in California provides a range of both adopted and homegrown intervention programs for struggling high school students. Among these programs are

- English classes that provide small-group, double-block classes for students who read significantly below grade level
- A double-block literacy program for students who need help with phonemic awareness, decoding, writing, and other literacy skills
- Literacy workshops for students who read two or more years below grade level and need help in acquiring reading comprehension and writing skills
- A two-period algebra class for students who need additional support
- A special class for students who failed the second semester of algebra the previous year
- Additional classes and Saturday tutoring for juniors and seniors who need extra help to master the skills needed to pass the California exit exam
- Intervention counselors
- Outlines that include suggestions for English language learners for every academic course offered

Examples of Successful Interventions

The staff at Jenks High School in Oklahoma, which is among the highest-achieving high schools in the state, provides additional reading and writing classes and algebra labs to students who need extra help in English or Algebra I. This structure has been significantly successful because the best teachers in the school are assigned to these extra support classes. Extra time with a weak teacher may do more harm than good, but extra time with an expert teacher is a winning combination.

The Center for Public Education's 2006 report *Making Time* provides cautious support for extended learning time and block scheduling as structures for intervening with and supporting struggling high school students. In the schools included in the study, the researchers found that extended learning time was most often used to double learning time in language arts and math and block scheduling with its longer class periods was used to increase opportunities to individualize instruction and address unique student learning needs.

Granger High School in Washington state, which includes a population of high-poverty, mostly minority students, attributes its dramatic increase in state test scores, graduation rates, and post-secondary education attendance rates to the addition of an advisory program, a locally-grown reading program, and a policy that allows students to retake failed quizzes and tests. Fruita Monument High School in Colorado developed one-, two-, and three-semester classes, a math lab, and common assessments to significantly reduce the number of students failing geometry at the school. Columbia Heights High School in Minnesota went from having no collective response to struggling students to implementing a schoolwide intervention plan that enables faculty and staff to get support quickly to struggling students. The staff at Columbia used an academic-focused advisory program; afterschool tutoring; and a three-week, afterschool, online credit completion program. Overall, failure rates have been reduced for students in all grades, with freshmen failure rates dropping by as much as 68 percent.

North Central High School in Spokane, Washington, changed the registration process from listing college-prep courses as electives to citing those same courses as the default curriculum. Additionally, faculty and staff members support the increased academic rigor for students with intense training, coaching, and implementation of constructivist teaching strategies. Their goal is to increase the number of graduates who are eligible to apply to four-year colleges from 37 to 75 percent.

Papillion-La Vista South High School in Nebraska reduced failure rates, particularly among special education students, by insisting that students complete assigned homework through a combination of during school, afterschool, evening, and Saturday mandatory study sessions. The school also offers a Homework Opportunity Club where students can get help from teachers, complete homework and take tests, and receive weekly credit checks and plans of improvement. The North East Independent School District in Texas went from having 10 schools that failed to make AYP to all schools making AYP in one year by focusing on timely intervention for special education students. This district credits its turnaround to having intervention plans for every student at risk of failing and implementing improvement plans for each campus, along with considerable professional development and capacity building support from its central office.

My own attempts to provide intervention and support to struggling students at Littleton High School were similar to the initiatives outlined above, and some were met with mixed results. While I was principal at the school, we experimented with giving students at risk of failing English or geometry extra instructional time. The school is on a modified block schedule wherein every class meets on Mondays for 46 minutes and again on Tuesdays and Thursdays or Wednesdays and Fridays for 90-minute blocks. Students who were capable of mastering the regular curriculum but needed additional time and support were assigned to an extra half block of instruction twice each week. The purpose of the schedule was to provide students with English or geometry classes every day instead of just three times each week. A few students benefited from the arrangement but not the majority. In hindsight, we might have been more successful had we been more selective about which teachers were scheduled into the labs and more structured and systematic about using common diagnostic and formative assessments to guide our remediation efforts.

In one of our other major efforts to mount a deliberate, collective response to student failure at Littleton, we established a Freshman Academy. Each year, we predicted that about 20 percent of our freshmen would finish the year with multiple *D*s and *F*s, which was our definition of a student "at risk." After tinkering with weekly progress checks, conferences with counselors and parents, and other attempts to try to change the student rather than change the school, we ended the year by confirming our prediction. In retrospect that sounds like professional malpractice—knowing something wouldn't work but doing it anyway.

We finally decided to do something bolder, and we created a school within a school for about 60 incoming 9th-grade students whose previous performance or early diagnostic assessments indicated they would likely fail in the regular curriculum and large school environment. The program of study at the Freshman Academy focused on literacy and math and provided students with twice as much instructional time than they would have received in the mainstream program. Students were also encouraged to take one elective course outside of the academy. Teachers were specially selected to staff the program.

The goal of the Freshman Academy was to equip students with literacy, math, and study skills, and the confidence they would need to be successful in the mainstream program as sophomores. When evaluated against that goal, the program has been only moderately successful. After the first year of implementation, about half of all sophomores who were in the program as freshmen had no *D*s or *F*s at the end of the first semester and another 25 percent had only one low grade. Those are not great numbers, but, remember that we are dealing with a population that is 100 percent at risk. Although attendance and passing rates remain strong for students while they are in the program, subsequent follow-up studies have yielded less promising figures for the success of Freshman Academy students as sophomores. I believe the problem is the lack of significant support for Freshman Academy graduates in grades 10–12. It is probably wishful to think that at-risk students can be "fixed" in one year.

Regardless of the strategies employed, there are several common elements within successful intervention programs. Those elements are captured in a recent report commissioned by the Bill & Melinda Gates Foundation, which analyzed the following similarities among five high-performing high school programs:

> Each program emphasizes college as an attainable goal, provides rigorous college-preparatory courses, establishes a well-designed curriculum for all grades, strengthens academic and social supports during the freshman year, and encourages out-of-school youths to return to the classroom. (Ash, 2007)

High school teachers are exhorted to differentiate instruction to reach students who do not respond well to whole-group instruction. Yet, few teachers express confidence in knowing how to do that, given their student loads and the structure of the traditional U.S. high school. Carol Ann Tomlinson (2008), recognized for her research and writing on this topic, recently identified several strategies for individualizing instruction:

1. Differentiation calls for teachers to have clear learning goals that are rooted in content standards but crafted to ensure student engagement and understanding.
2. [Teachers] use rubrics that are carefully constructed to support student thinking about the quality of their work instead of merely awarding points for completed work.

3. Further, differentiation calls on teachers to vigilantly monitor student proximity to content goals throughout a learning cycle.
4. They have students keep track of their own skill development, feedback, and grades.
5. [Teachers who differentiate] adapt teaching plans to attend to learner readiness, interest, and preferred modes of learning.

Notice any similarities between what Tomlinson recommends and the 6+1 Model for High School Reform? Strategy 1 calls for clear learning goals. Strategies 2 and 3 recommend that teachers monitor student progress using rubrics and formative assessments. Tracking student progress is the focus of strategy 4, and strategy 5 asks teachers to personalize instruction as both a preventative and an intervention strategy. Making these connections can help high school teachers demystify differentiated instruction.

Just as it does no good to find out that students are struggling with essential content and skills after instruction is over, it makes no sense to create rubrics, and use formative assessment and then ignore the results. Deliberate, collective, focused timely intervention is essential for great high schools. Although timely intervention is perhaps the most challenging of all of the good-to-great strategies to design and implement successfully, we can take heart in and learn from the experiences of high schools across the country that have taken on that challenge.

8

Strategy 6: Celebrating Student Success

The final strategy in the 6+1 Model for High School Reform, celebrating student success, brings closure to the progression of strategies that constitute the model and reinforces the previous strategies on self-efficacy, motivation, and engagement. After tracking student progress on important learning goals and intervening as necessary on results from formative assessment, students, teachers, and entire faculties should be invited to celebrate success as it becomes evident and sustained.

It is satisfying to see that one's hard work has paid off, and that sense of satisfaction translates into continued engagement and increased levels of self-efficacy for both students and teachers. Individual students should be recognized for achieving personal learning goals, and teachers and teacher teams should be recognized for reaching class, course-level, or school goals. But, as is the case with most things in education, there are things to be learned from research about ways to celebrate success that produce long-term, positive results.

Background Research on Providing Recognition

There is disagreement across the research community regarding the long-term effects of recognition and rewards on the development of both cognitive and life skills in children. Arguably, the most renowned critic of many frequently used methods of recognizing and rewarding student achievement and behavior is Alfie Kohn. In short, Kohn argues that while manipulating people with rewards seems to work in the short run, the strategy fails in the long run by actually lowering both intrinsic motivation and the quality of work produced (Kohn, 1999, 2005, 2008). There is also disagreement within the research community about proposed plans to pay students for high scores on AP and state accountability tests in Arizona, California, New York, Ohio, and other states ("Cash for grades, 2007; Lou, 2007; Medina, 2007, June 19; Medina, 2007, October 15; Saul & Einhorn, 2007; Steiny, 2008; Viadero, 2007, January 17). In their meta-analysis, Marzano and colleagues (2001) generated the following generalizations from the research on recognition.

1. *Rewards do not necessarily have a negative effect on intrinsic motivation.* Marzano and colleagues caution us that it is important to distinguish between rewards, praise, and recognition. They also admonish us to identify the dependent variable used to determine the effect of the reward when examining research results on these strategies. When the effects of rewards are measured by students' ability to perform the rewarded activity, effect sizes are moderately strong.

2. *A reward is most effective when it is contingent on the attainment of some standard of performance.* Rewarding students simply for completing an activity does not enhance intrinsic motivation. Under such circumstances, students could develop the idea that they have to get paid to do their work. When students are offered rewards for the successful attainment of a specific performance goal, this enhances their intrinsic motivation. In connection with this generalization, Marzano and colleagues emphasize that recognition should be personalized whenever possible through strategies such as establishing a "personal best" honor roll. This conclusion suggests that the pay-for-performance plans mentioned earlier might have positive effects on learning.

3. *Abstract symbolic recognition is more effective than tangible rewards.* Verbal rewards often work better than candy or money. For a decade, Seymour High School in Indiana has celebrated success with an Academic Convocation celebration for students who earn a ticket to go. Students must achieve academically, behave responsibly at school, and have good attendance to earn a ticket. The celebration is a variety show of sorts, featuring performances by students, teachers, and administrators. This symbolic recognition event has become a cherished tradition in the school (McClure, 2007).

When teachers give verbal rewards or praise to students for effort instead of intelligence, the students are more likely to be in a mindset for growth. For example, when a teacher gives a verbal reward such as, "Wendy, you've been working hard on your fluency, and your last essay shows it," this type of recognition is more effective than saying, "John, you must have been born with the writing gene." In one study, students who were praised for intelligence were more likely to lose their confidence when they began to struggle to and to falsify their results than students who were rewarded for effort (Dweck, 2007). Figure 8.1 shows examples and offers guidance on effectively using verbal rewards with students.

Figure 8.1
Guidelines for Praise

Effective Praise . . .	**Ineffective Praise . . .**
1. Is delivered contingently.	1. Is delivered randomly or unsystematically.
2. Specifies the particulars of the accomplishment.	2. Is restricted to global positive reactions.
3. Shows spontaneity, variety, and other signs of credibility; suggests clear attention to the students' accomplishments.	3. Shows a bland uniformity that suggests a conditional response made with minimal attention.
4. Rewards attainment of specified performance criteria (which can include effort criteria).	4. Rewards mere participation, without consideration of performance, processes, or outcomes.
5. Provides information to students about their competence or the value of their accomplishments.	5. Provides no information at all or gives students no information about their status.
6. Orients students toward better appreciation of their own task-related behavior and thinking about problem solving.	6. Orients students toward comparing themselves with others and thinking about competing.
7. Uses students' own prior accomplishments as the context for describing present accomplishments.	7. Uses the accomplishments of peers as the context for describing students' present accomplishments.
8. Is given in recognition of noteworthy effort or success at difficult (for *this* student) tasks.	8. Is given without regard to the effort expended or the meaning of the accomplishment.
9. Attributes success to effort and ability, implying that similar successes can be expected in the future.	9. Attributes success to ability alone or to external factors such as luck or low task difficulty.
10. Fosters endogenous attributions (students believe that they expend effort on the task because they enjoy the task and/or want to develop task-relevant skills).	10. Fosters exogenous attributions (students believe that they expend effort on the task for external reasons — to please the teacher, win a competition or reward, etc.).
11. Focuses students' attention on their own task-relevant behavior.	11. Focuses students' attention on the teacher as an external authority who is manipulating them.
12. Fosters appreciation of, and desirable attributions about, task-relevant behavior after the process is completed.	12. Intrudes into the ongoing process, distracting attention from task-relevant behavior.

Source: *Classroom Instruction That Works* (p. 56), by R. Marzano, D. Pickering, & J. Pollock, 2001, Alexandria, VA: ASCD Adapted with permission.

Publicly displaying student work has long been a strategy for recognizing students' accomplishments at the elementary level, but this strategy has not yet found its way into many high schools. High school students, however, often do their best work when they know it will be seen by someone of importance besides their teachers. Witness the effort students put into science fairs, student newspapers, art shows, music or theater performances, and sporting events. Ownership increases when student work is open to public review.

Technology now offers a convenient and effective way to display student work by enabling students to post their work on Web sites. For example, all students at New Technology High School in Napa, California, are required to post student work portfolios online (Pitler, Hubbell, Kuhn, & Malenoski, 2007).

Celebrating Success with Students

Celebrating success happens in a variety of ways. Two specific examples, one for students and one for teachers, come to mind from my experiences at Littleton High School.

Honor rolls have long been used in high schools to recognize academic achievement. In most cases, grade point or percentage cutoffs are established for various categories of distinction, for example, some schools use distinctions like "honors" and "high honor" or color categories like "purple" and "gold." Students who meet the criteria are recognized in various ways, including having their names published in school or community newsletters and newspapers and being recognized at school assemblies. A few schools even offer students prizes and cash awards in recognition for academic excellence.

Littleton High School has had such a program in place for decades. Each semester, the names of students who achieve honors (3.0–3.4 GPA), high honors (3.5–3.7 GPA), and highest honors (3.8 GPA and above) are posted at the school and in the school newspaper. Students are pleased and parents are thrilled. There is nothing wrong with such practices, except that honor rolls, as traditionally defined, tend to recognize those students who need praise the least. In most cases, these high-achieving students have always done well in school and most likely receive recognition for their accomplishments in multiple forms at home and school. But what about recognition for students who do not have extremely high grade point averages or percentages yet are working hard and improving each semester?

Several years ago, the staff at Littleton created a Most Improved Honor Roll to recognize those students who had the biggest increases in their grade point averages. This strategy is aligned with the effort-based learning philosophy outlined in Chapter 2, and it helps teachers to celebrate students who are working hard and getting better. This strategy is especially successful for students who had a bad start early in their high school careers. For example, a student who raised his or her grade point average from 1.5 to 2.5 was recognized for his or her accomplishments, even though the overall GPA was far from the level needed to receive an honors distinction.

The Most Improved recognition program was eventually discontinued due largely to our lack of awareness of the importance of recognizing effort-based learning. Our knowledge today of motivation theory and research suggests that such programs for celebrating success merit a second look.

Celebrating Success with Teachers and Staff

People on the payroll need opportunities to celebrate success as well. Celebrating success for teachers, administrators, and staff members can happen in a variety of different, and sometimes unexpected, ways.

I was having dinner at a local restaurant after a basketball game late one evening when the parents of two successful graduates of our school walked in and joined me. The family had moved to our community from out of state when both children were in high school, and they were quite concerned about the transition. What came out of that dinner conversation was a truly unusual opportunity to celebrate the success our school and particularly our teachers had with those two students. These parents appreciated the personal attention, deep content knowledge, and quality of instruction that their children received at Littleton. They believed that these qualities prepared their children to excel in college. That evening the family made arrangements to give Littleton $100,000 to be used specifically to recognize and ensure quality teaching at the school. Talk about being ready to celebrate. I could not wait to share the news with the faculty. But how would I do that? Surely something more than a standard announcement at a faculty meeting was in order.

With assistance from my administrative team, we found two ways to use this opportunity to celebrate success. At the next faculty meeting, teachers were given $100,000 candy bars, without explanation, as they entered the room.

Speculation ran wild. At the end of the meeting, with an oh-by-the-way air, we brought out a giant mock check and announced the news. Words cannot adequately describe how we all felt as we left the room that day. This was phase one of celebrating our success.

Phase two of the celebration was an all-expenses paid, overnight retreat for the entire faculty to a well-known Colorado resort the following fall, which was paid for by proceeds from the family gift. The two-day event was a well-structured professional development and planning retreat, but it was impossible to forget that we were not in the school cafeteria. We worked hard and we celebrated our success hard. I cannot tell you how many times I heard participants utter some form of "We're finally being treated like professionals."

You don't have to wait for a large financial gift to roll in to celebrate success with your colleagues. That event was a once-in-a-lifetime event; however, opportunities to recognize accomplishments and celebrate success present themselves to us on an almost daily basis. Take the time to see them and seize them.

Celebrating Success by Using Technology

Earlier in this chapter, I briefly mentioned the potential of emerging technology to help teachers recognize student achievement and celebrate success. I read an article in *The New York Times* about a music teacher in a school on Staten Island who posts videos of his students' performances on the Internet via a You Tube channel that he created for the students (Ensha, 2008). He also updates information about the students' performances on a complementary blog. When the teacher posted a performance from his students that featured a song by Tori Amos, the singer watched the video and invited the students to perform the song with her in midtown Manhattan. You can imagine what a thrill that must have been for those students and their teacher. It's no doubt that these students work hard to perfect their craft knowing that their performances are available for the whole world to see.

Schools around the country are experimenting with ways to use technology to recognize achievement and increase student engagement. For example, Fox Chapel School District in Pennsylvania is participating in a state pilot for using an offshoot of Apple's digital music jukebox to post student-generated original content on the Web. The depth of possibilities for recognition and celebration are unfathomable. We all strive to do our best work when we know it will be reviewed by people we respect and admire. Emerging technologies give us the ability to celebrate our success with the world.

Effectively using verbal recognition, focusing on performance standards and effort rather than task completion and intelligence, celebrating students through symbolic recognition events, putting student work on display, and personalizing feedback are important components of celebrating success. Celebrating what's right gives us the strength to fix what's wrong.

The 6+1 Model for High School Reform unfolds over time through a process that resembles what Robert Marzano (2007) has identified in the following six action steps:

1. Make a distinction between learning goals versus learning activities or assignments.
2. Write a rubric or scale for each learning goal.
3. Have students identify their own learning goals.
4. Assess students using a formative approach.
5. Have students chart their progress on each goal.
6. Recognize and celebrate growth. (pp. 17–28)

These building blocks of high performance must be assembled in the context of a we-expect-success culture to realize their full impact. The process for moving a school from good to great is like an elegant math proof: simple yet powerful.

AFTERWORD

I wanted to end the book with two final observations on capacity building and the scary process often referred to as second-order change.

Building Your School's Capacity for the 6+1 Model

School leadership teams have to decide how much of the 6+1 Model for High School Reform they have the capacity to take on. First, there is the issue of building and district leadership. Substantial evidence supports the commonsense conclusion that when it comes to improving student achievement, leadership matters (Marzano, 2008). Implementing the 6+1 Model for High School Reform requires extraordinary leadership from building and district administrators who know instruction, embrace effective schools research, and have a vision for high school education in the 21st century. These leaders also need to be well versed in organizational change theory, ready to devote financial and human resources to developing capacity, and willing to risk the political liabilities that often accompany moving a school from good to great. Such leadership is not in place in every school and district in the country. Visionaries interested in creating great high schools would be wise to assess building and district leadership capacity before deciding on how much or which parts of the model to take on.

Teacher leadership also needs to be considered. Effective administrative leadership at the building and district levels is essential, but it is not a sufficient resource for creating a great high school. In the truly great high schools in this country, teachers have the most important leadership roles—monitoring and improving the quality of instruction for students. High schools will never rise to the next level in today's political climate if quality control continues to be the responsibility of administrators, school boards, state legislators, governors, Congress, or the president. In my previous book, I review characteristics of professions and offer several alternative versions of a new vision of teacher leadership that can be used to spark discussion among teachers and administrators at the school or district level (Westerberg, 2007). Among other things, professionals

- Act on the most current knowledge in their field
- Are results-oriented
- Are client-centered and adapt to meet the needs of individuals
- Seek to foster productive client behaviors rather than to mandate compliance
- Improve their practice
- Improve common or collective practice in the profession
- Uphold agreed-upon standards of practice and specific protocols for performance

Together, these characteristics suggest that teachers, as professionals, have a responsibility to take charge of school improvement efforts.

I am heartened by the message of an open letter to the National Board of Certified Teachers. Ten National Board Certified teachers issued the following statement in a Teachers Solutions report about teachers' roles in improving America's schools (Flanagan et al., 2008):

> We believe National Board Certified Teachers (NBCTs) are uniquely positioned to challenge this outdated perception of teachers as mere instruments of policy and not co-creators. It is time for NBCTs to use what we know, as exemplary teachers, to lead our schools, colleagues, and policymakers toward more effective decisions and practices focused on genuine student learning. (p. 14)

Amen! For high schools to move from good to great, teaching must become a genuine profession rather than just a collection of individual professionals. It is important for people inside the profession to take responsibility for quality control. The Center for Teacher Quality in Hillsborough, North Carolina, is an excellent resource for teachers wishing to explore new definitions of teacher leadership (see www.teachingquality.org for more details).

Implementing Second-Order Change in Your School

School leadership teams also need to consider the difficult decision of whether or not to take on change at all. This decision can be especially difficult if the changes require players to rethink their basic assumptions, practices, and mental schemas about how high schools work.

Marzano and colleagues (2005) offer insight into why second-order change is so difficult. According to these researchers, second-order change is perceived as a break with the past, lies outside existing paradigms, often conflicts with prevailing values and norms, requires the acquisition of new knowledge and skills, and is not seen by many in the organization as necessary. The school's culture, modes of communication, sense of order, and opportunities for input are also perceived to be disrupted. It is easy to see why change of this nature is threatening and likely to be resisted by at least some members of a school's faculty and staff.

School principals and other members of the school's leadership team must first determine whether the school has the capacity and the culture necessary to support and sustain second-order change. If the staff capacity is limited and the culture is too toxic to change, work must be done in these arenas before taking on a second-order change. If these foundational elements are in place, specific leadership responsibilities must be emphasized and broadly distributed throughout a strong leadership team. According to Marzano and colleagues (2005), leadership responsibilities that are particularly important to second-order change include

- Possessing a knowledge of curriculum, instruction, and assessment related to the particular change being considered
- Inspiring and leading (the cheerleader) new and challenging innovations
- Ensuring that faculty and staff members are aware of the most current theories and practices and making the discussion of these topics a regular aspect of the school's culture
- Actively challenging the status quo
- Monitoring the effectiveness of school practices and their impact on student learning
- Modeling flexibility, adaptability, and a high comfort level with dissent
- Communicating and operating from strong ideals and beliefs about schooling. (pp. 42–43, 70)

If the capacity to meet these responsibilities is lacking, school leaders should add members to the leadership team who possess the knowledge, skill, or dispositions needed. They should also make it a top priority to develop the missing knowledge, skills, and dispositions among existing team members.

One thing I am pretty sure of is that there are only two ways to improve results—redesign your school based on best practices or get different kids. If you have the option of getting different kids, I suggest you do that. Perhaps you could send a letter home to parents asking them to send their *other* kids to school. If you do that, you would not have to think about second-order change and all of this 6+1 stuff. But, if that is not an option for you, and if you have a mission to serve whoever shows up at the schoolhouse door each morning, you only have one alternative—improve your school.

A few years ago, I adapted the following quotation to reflect what I consider to be the leadership challenge in high school education:

> Leadership in today's high schools is not a journey to retirement with the intention of arriving safely, without risk, with all that is now familiar intact, but rather to skid in broadside, thoroughly used up, totally worn out, and loudly proclaiming, "Wow, we've closed some gaps between best practice and common practice. What a ride!" (Author unknown)

We can defend what we have or create what we want. How do you want to spend your time?

References

Aguerrebere, J. A., Houston, P. D., & Tirozzi, G. N. (2007, December 12). Toward the 'highly qualified' principal. *Education Week, 27*(15), 28, 36.

Arenson, K. W. (2007, October 24). Program to deter high school dropouts by offering college courses is approved. *The New York Times.*

Ash, K. (2007, June 23). Core curriculum seen falling short. *Education Week, 26*(38).

Ash, K. (2007, September 26). College readiness. *Education Week, 27*(5), 4–5.

Bambrick-Santoyo, P. (2007–08, December–January). Data in the driver's seat. *Educational Leadership, 65*(4), 43–46.

Baron, D. (2007, February). Using text-based protocols: The five Rs. *Principal Leadership, 7*(6), 50–51.

Bassett, P. F. (2008, February 20). What the Finns know shouldn't surprise us (but does). *Education Week, 27*(24), 28–29.

Berger, J. (2007, March 7). Intel competition is where science rules and research is the key. *The New York Times*, B7.

Berry, B. (2004, July 12). Finding your purpose: At home, at work and in the community. Keynote address at the Principals' Partnership 2004 Summer Leadership Institute.

Black, P., & Wiliam, D. (1998, March). Assessment and classroom learning. *Assessment in Education, 5*(1),7–74.

Boone, E., Hartzman, M., Mero, D., & Rourke, J. (2008, June). Breakthrough schools: Case studies from the MetLife Foundation—NASSP breakthrough schools. *Principal Leadership, Special Edition.*

Calkins, A., Guenther, W., Belfiore, G., & Lash, D. (2007). *The turnaround challenge: Why America's best opportunity to dramatically improve student achievement lies in our worst-performing schools.* Boston, MA: Mass Insight Education & Research Institute. Retrieved February 5, 2009, from http://www.massinsight.org/resourcefiles/TheTurnaroundChallenge_2007.pdf

Cash for grades? An odd idea whose time may have come. (2007, August 17). *USA Today*, p. 10A. Retrieved February 5, 2009, from http://www.usatoday.com/printedition/news/20070817/edit17.art.htm

Cavanagh, S. (2007, October 17). Math and science ventures to be scaled up. *Education Week, 27* (8), 8.

Cavanagh, S. (2007, December 12). Poverty's effect on U.S. scores greater than for other nations. *Education Week, 27*(15), 1, 13.

Cavanagh, S. (2008, February 6). MIT orients course material online to K–12. *Education Week, 27*(22), 1, 13.

Cavanagh, S. (2008, March 27). States heeding calls to strengthen STEM. *Education Week, 27*(30), 10, 12–13, 16, 22–23.

Cech, S. J. (2008, February 20). AP trends: Tests soar, scores slip. *Education Week, 27*(24), 1, 13.

Cech, S. J. (2008, September 17). Test industry split over 'formative' assessment. *Education Week, 28*(4), 1, 15.

The Center for Public Education. (2006, September 25). Making time: What research says about re-organizing school schedules. Alexandria, VA: Author. Retrieved February 5, 2009, from http://www.centerforpubliceducation.org/site/c.kjJXJ5MPIwE/b.2086551/k.9967/Making_time_What_research_says_about_reorganizing_school_schedules.htm

Christie, K. (2007, September). Stateline. *Phi Delta Kappan, 89*(1), 5–6.

Chute, E. (2007, June 3). In high schools, a 'B' is the new 'C.' *Pittsburgh Post-Gazette*. Retrieved February 9, 2009, from http://www.post-gazette.com/pg/07154/791202-298.stm

Conley, D. (2005, September). College knowledge: Getting in is only half the battle. *Principal Leadership, 6*(1), 16–21.

Corbett, G. C., & Huebner, T. A. (2007). *Rethinking high school: Preparing students for college, career, and life*. San Francisco: WestEd.

Craig, J. (2003, November). Beyond the rock and the hard place. *Educational Leadership, 61(3)*, 12–16.

Dalton, R., & Mills, J. (2008, September 3). Lost horizons: Making college a reality for rural students. *Education Week, 28*(2), 26–27.

Darling-Hammond, L., & Friedlaender, D. (2008, May). Creating excellent and equitable schools. *Educational Leadership, 65*(8), 14–21.

Davis, G. (2007, August 11). System charts pupil progress: Baltimore County tests computerized checklist for parents. *The Baltimore Sun*. Retrieved February 9, 2009, from www.baltimoresun.com/news/local/baltimore_county/bal-te.md.co.progress11aug11,0,1022410.story

de Vise, D. (2007, March 25). To be AP, courses must pass muster. *The Washington Post*, A01.

de Vise, D. (2008, May 16). Honors courses give way to AP rigor. *The Washington Post*, B01.

DeWitt, S. (2008, April). Blurring the lines: Career and technical education today. *Principal Leadership, 8*(8), 16–21.

DuFour, R. (2008, July 15). *Managers do things right: Leaders do the right things*. Keynote address at the Union Pacific Corporation Summer Leadership Institute, Palm Desert, CA.

DuFour, R., & DuFour, B. (2004, September 29). *Professional learning communities*. Workshop presented in Denver, CO.

DuFour, R., Eaker, R., & DuFour, R. (2005). *On common ground*. Bloomington, IN: National Educational Service.

Dweck, C. S. (2007, October). The perils and promise of praise. *Educational Leadership, 65*(2), 34–39.

Elmore, R. F. (2003, November). A plea for strong practice. *Educational Leadership, 61*,(3), 6–10.

Ensha, A. (2008, December 26). Staten Island school chorus finds fame on YouTube. *The New York Times*, A28.

Farrace, R. (2008, April). Double duty. *Principal Leadership, 8*(8), 22–26.

Finalists named for 2009 national principal of the year awards. (2008, September). *Newsleader, 56*(1), 2, 11.

Fischer, K. (2008, August 15). Teachers give Dallas ISD's new grading rules an F. *The Dallas Morning News*. Available from http://www.dallasnews.com/sharedcontent/dws/news/localnews/stories/DN-DISDgrades_15met.ART.State.Edition2.4d95d34.html

Fisher, D., & Frey, N. (2008). *Better learning through structured teaching.* Alexandria, VA: ASCD.

Flanagan, N., Cody, A., Graham, S., Holmes, E., Kuemmel, A., Ledesma, P., et al. (2008). Measuring what matters: The effects of National Board Certification on advancing 21st century teaching and learning. Hillsborough, NC: Center for Teaching Quality. Retrieved February 5, 2009, from http://www.teachingquality.org/legacy/MeasuringWhatMatters.pdf

Fuchs, L. S., & Fuchs, D. (1986). Effects of systematic formative evaluation: A meta-analysis. *Exceptional Children, 53*(3), 199–208.

Fullan, M. (2006). *Turnaround leadership.* San Francisco: Jossey-Bass.

Fullan, M. (2007, August 2). Keynote address at the 38th Annual CASE Convention, Breckenridge, CO.

Fullan, M. (2008). *The six secrets of change*. San Francisco: Jossey-Bass.

Gearino, D. (2007, December 31). Students: Still in high school, but also taking college classes. *Quad-City Times*.

Gewertz, C. (2007, June 12). 'Soft skills' in big demand. *Education Week, 26*(40), 25–27.

Goldberg, S. (2008, January). *Beating the odds: The real challenges behind the math achievement gap—and what high-achieving schools can teach us about how to close it.* [Executive summary]. Boston: Jobs for the Future.

Grubb, W. N., & Oakes, J. (2007, October). 'Restoring value' to the high school diploma: The rhetoric and practice of higher standards. Boulder, CO: Arizona State University Education and the Public Interest Center.

Hattie, J. A. (1999, June). Influences on student learning. (Inaugural professorial address, University of Auckland, New Zealand). Retrieved from http://web.auckland.ac.nz/uoa/fms/default/education/staff/Prof.%20John%20Hattie/Documents/Presentations/influences/Influences_on_student_learning.pdf

Hattie, J., & Timperley, H. (2007). The power of feedback. *Review of Educational Research, 77*(1), 81–112.

Hirsh, S., & Killion, J. (2008, April 16). Making every educator a learning educator. *Education Week, 27*(33), 24–25.

Hoachlander, G. (2008, May). Bringing industry to the classroom. *Educational Leadership, 65*(8), 22–27.

Hoff, D. (2008, June 18). Bell curve author to question college goal in new book. *Education Week, 27*(42), 14.

Honawar, V. (2008, April 2). Working smarter by working together. *Education Week, 27*(31), 25–27.

Housman, N. G., Muller, R. D., & Chait, R. (2006, October). Increasing academic rigor in high schools: Stakeholder perspectives. Washington, DC: Institute for Educational Leadership. Retrieved February 5, 2009, from http://www.hsalliance.org/_downloads/NNCO/RigorScan.pdf

Huebner, T. A., & Corbett, G. C. (2008). *Rethinking high school: Supporting all students to be college-ready in math.* San Francisco: WestEd.

Jalongo, M. R. (2007). Beyond benchmarks and scores: Reasserting the role of motivation and interest in children's academic achievement [Position paper]. Olney, MD: Association for Childhood Education International.

Johnson, S. M., & Donaldson, M. L. (2007, September). Overcoming the obstacles to leadership. *Educational Leadership, 65*(1), 8–13.

Kay, K., & Houlihan, G.T. (2006, May 17). Redefining 'rigor' for a new century. *Education Week, 25* (37), 31, 33.

Kennedy-Manzo, K. (2007, February 28). Students taking more demanding courses. *Education Week, 26*(25), 1, 17.

Klein, A. (2007, February 7). Researchers see college benefits for students who took AP courses. *Education Week, 26*(22), 7.

Kohn, A. (1999). *Punished by rewards: The trouble with gold stars, incentive plans, As, praise, and other bribes.* Boston: Houghton Mifflin.

Kohn, A. (2005). *Unconditional parenting.* New York: Simon & Schuster.

Kohn, A. (2008, September 10). It's not what we teach, it's what they learn. *Education Week, 28* (3), 32, 26.

Landsberg, M. (2007, February 22). Study says students are learning less. *The Los Angeles Times,* A14.

Lou, L. (2007, March 28). Rewards for high scores. *SignOnSanDiego.com.* Retrieved February 9, 2009, from http://www.signonsandiego.com/news/education/20070328-9999-1mi28smgrade.html

Marklein, M. B. (2007, April 9). Schoolteachers, professors differ on what students should know. *USA Today.* Retrieved February 9, 2009, from http://www.usatoday.com/news/education/2007-04-09-teachers-professors-differ_n.htm

Marshall, K. (2006, September 20). What's a principal to do? *Education Week, 26*(4), 36–37.

Marshall, K. (2008, March). The big rocks: Priority management for principals. *Principal Leadership, 8*(7), 16–22.

Marzano, R. J. (2003). *What works in schools: Translating research into action.* Alexandria, VA: ASCD.

Marzano, R. J. (2006). *Classroom assessment and grading that work.* Alexandria, VA: ASCD.

Marzano, R. J. (2007). *The art and science of teaching.* Alexandria, VA: ASCD.

Marzano, R. J. (2008). *Getting serious about school reform: Three critical commitments.* Bloomington, IN: Solution Tree.

Marzano, R. J., & Haystead, M. W. (2008). *Making standards useful in the classroom.* Alexandria, VA: ASCD.

Marzano, R. J., & Kendall, J. S. (2008). *Designing & assessing educational objectives: Applying the new taxonomy.* Thousand Oaks, CA: Corwin Press.

Marzano, R. J., Pickering, D. J., & Pollock, J. E. (2001). *Classroom instruction that works.* Alexandria, VA: ASCD.

Marzano, R. J., Waters, T., & McNulty, B. (2005). *School leadership that works: From research to results.* Alexandria, VA: ASCD.

Mathews, J. (2006, September 19). In many classrooms, 'honors' in name only. *The Washington Post,* A10.

Mathews, J. (2007, December 27). Grading disparities peeve parents. *The Washington Post,* A01.

Mathews, J. (2008, April 14). Embracing the challenge of AP English for all students. *The Washington Post,* B2.

McClure, D. (2007, April). A ticket to the show. *Principal Leadership, 8*(8), 60.

Medina, J. (2007, June 19). Schools plan to pay cash for marks. *The New York Times*. Retrieved February 9, 2009, from http://www.nytimes.com/2007/06/19/nyregion/19schools.html?_r=1&oref=slogin&papewa&oref=slogin

Medina, J. (2007, October 15). Making cash a prize for high scores on advanced placement tests. *The New York Times*. Retrieved February 9, 2009, from http://www.nytimes.com/2007/10/15/nyregion/15rewards.html?_r=1&oref=slogin&page

Mellon, E. (2008, May 22). Courses give some a college try. *Houston Chronicle*.

Mitchell Institute. (2007). From high school to college: Removing barriers for Maine students—A summary. Portland, ME: Author

Nagel, D. (2008, March). Giving high school students more time. *Principal Leadership, 8*(7), 29–31.

National Association of Secondary School Principals. (2004). *Breaking ranks II: Strategies for leading high school reform*. Reston, VA: Author.

National Mathematics Advisory Panel. (2008, March). *Foundations for success: The final report of the National Mathematics Advisory Panel*. Washington, DC: U.S. Department of Education. Retrieved February 5, 2009, from http://www.ed.gov/about/bdscomm/list/mathpanel/report/final-report.pdf

Nemko, M. (2008, May 25). Overrated: College diploma. *The Dallas Morning News*. Retrieved February 9, 2009, from http://www.dallasnews.com/sharedcontent/dws/dn/opinion/points/stories/DN-nemko_25edi.ART0.State.Edition1.465abff.html

Newell, R. J., & Van Ryzin, M. J. (2007, February). Growing hope as a determinant of school effectiveness. *Phi Delta Kappan, 88*(6), 465–471.

Noddings, N. (2007, March 20). The new anti-intellectualism in America. *Education Week, 26*(28), 29, 32.

Northwest Regional Educational Laboratory. (2006, September). Finding time for collaboration. *Principal's Research Review, 1*(5). Portland, OR: Author. Retrieved February 5, 2009, from http://www.nwrel.org/csdi/services/plt/Tools/FindingTime.pdf

Olson, L. (2007, April 18). Policy push redefining high school. *Education Week, 26*(33), 1, 20.

Olson, L. (2008, January 16). Assessment to rate principal leadership to be field-tested. *Education Week, 27*(19), 1, 11.

Pianta, R. C. (2007, November 7). Measure actual classroom teaching. *Education Week, 27*(11), 36, 30.

Pitler, H., Hubbell, E. R., Kuhn, M., & Malenoski, K. (2007). *Using technology with classroom instruction that works*. Alexandria, VA: ASCD; and Denver, CO: McRel.

Popham, W. J. (2008). *Transformative assessment*. Alexandria, VA: ASCD.

Recent state policies/activities: High school-grad requirements. (2007). Denver, CO: Education Commission of the States. Retrieved February 5, 2009, from http://www.ecs.org/ecs/ecscat.nsf/WebTopicView?OpenView&count=300&RestrictToCategory=High+School-Grad+Requirements

Reeves, D. B. (2001). *101 questions and answers about standards, assessments, and accountability*. Denver, CO: Advanced Learning Centers.

Reeves, D. B. (2006). *The learning leader*. Alexandria, VA: ASCD.

Reeves, D. B. (2008). *Reframing teacher leadership*. Alexandria, VA: ASCD.

Reeves, D. B. (2008, April). The leadership challenge in literacy. *Educational Leadership, 65*(7), 91–92.

Rigor/relevance framework. (n.d.). Rexford, NY: International Center for Leadership in Education. Retrieved February 5, 2009, from http://www.daggett.com/rigor.html

Roderick, M., Nagaoka, J., & Allensworth, E. (2008, March). From high school to the future. Chicago: Consortium on Chicago School Research, University of Chicago.

Rolph, A. (2008, March 23). Good pay, steady work, few takers as young people spurn the trades. *Seattle Post-Intelligencer.* Retrieved February 9, 2009, from http://seattlepi.nwsource.com/business/356181_trades24.html

Rossi, L. (2007, March 5). More high schoolers tackle college courses. *The Des Moines Register,* 1A, 4A.

Roth, L. (2008, March 2). Beach students receive industry certificates. *The Virginian Pilot.* Retrieved February 9, 2009, from http://hamptonroads.com/node/456169

Roth, M. (2007, November 26). Student success tied to teacher mentoring. *Pittsburgh Post-Gazette.* Retrieved February 9, 2009, from http://www.post-gazette.com/pg/07330/836795-85.stm

Rourke, J. R. (2007, November). Leveraging resources to close the divide. *Principal Leadership, 8*(3), 24–25.

Saifer, S., & Barton, R. (2007, September). Promoting culturally responsive standards-based teaching. *Principal Leadership, 8*(1), 24–28.

Saul, M., & Einhorn, E. (2007, June 9). Cash is cool: Mike. *New York Daily News,* 8.

Schmoker, M. (2006). *Results now: How we can achieve unprecedented improvements in teaching and learning.* Alexandria, VA: ASCD.

Schmoker, M. (2007, June 14). Keynote address at the CASE New Century Schools Summit, Breckenridge, CO.

Shields, R. A., & Hawley-Miles, K. (2008). *Strategic designs: Lessons from leading edge small urban high schools.* Watertown, MA: Education Resource Strategies.

Smydo, J. (2008, September 22). Eyebrows raised over city school policy that sets 50% as minimum score. *Pittsburgh Post-Gazette.* Retrieved February 9, 2009, from http://www.post-gazette.com/pg/08266/914029-298.stm

Steiny, J. (2008, September 7). Bribing kids to pass tests is a sad comment on schools. *The Providence Journal.* Retrieved February 9, 2009, http://www.projo.com/education/juliasteiny/content/se_educationwatch07_09-07-08_8LBETHN_v8.5ba76a.html

Stiggins, R. (2004, September). New assessment beliefs for a new school mission. *Phi Delta Kappan, 86*(1), 22–27.

Stiggins, R. (2007, May). Assessment through the student's eyes. *Educational Leadership, 64*(8), 22–26.

Stiggins, R. (2008, April). Assessment manifesto: A call for the development of balanced assessment systems. Presentation at ETS Assessment Training Institute, Portland, OR.

Strepp, D.R. (2007, December 14). A formula for higher learning. Taking on college math early, teens tune in to Georgia Tech. *The Atlanta Journal-Constitution,* E1.

Supovitz, J. (2007, November 28). Why we need district-based reform. *Education Week, 27*(13), 27–28.

Swanson, J. (2007, March). Dual enrollment and advanced placement: Partners for student success. *Principal Leadership, 7*(7), 26–30.

The 10-point plan. (n.d.). Washington, DC: America's Promise Alliance. Retrieved February 5, 2009, from http://www.americaspromise.org/APAPage.aspx?id=9176&terms=10-Point+Plan+for+reducing+Dropout+rate

Toch, T., Jerald, C. D., & Dillon, E. (2007, February). Surprise—high school reform is working. *Phi Delta Kappan, 88*(7), 433–437.

Tomlinson, C. A. (2008, November). The goals of differentiation. *Educational Leadership, 66*(3), 26–30.

Tracking the reasons many girls avoid science and math. (2008, September 8). *ScienceDaily.* Retrieved February 5, 2009, from http://www.sciencedaily.com/releases/2008/09/080905153807.htm

Trotter, A. (2008, March 27). A school where STEM is king. *Education Week, 27*(30), 24–26.

Umphrey, J. (2008, January). Producing learning: A conversation with Robert Marzano. *Principal Leadership,8*(5), 16–20.

University of Oklahoma. (2008, June 30). Attitude determines student success in rural schools. *Science Daily.* Retrieved February 5, 2009, from http://www.sciencedaily.com/releases/2008/06/080619174221.htm

Using assessment to motivate students. (1997). *Education Update, 39*(8). Retrieved February 5, 2009, from http://www.ascd.org/publications/newsletters/education_update/dec97/vol39/num08/Using_Assessment_to_Motivate_Students.aspx

Vance, B. K. (2008, January 30). Glenpool ZAPs homework issue. *Tulsa World.* Retrieved February 5, 2009, from http://www.tulsaworld.com/news/articleaspx?articleID=20080130_9_ZS3_spanc55567

Viadero, D. (2006, August 30). Cognitive studies offer insights on academic tactic. *Education Week, 26*(1), 12–13.

Viadero, D. (2007, October 24). Experiments aim to ease effects of 'stereotype threat.' *Education Week, 26*(9), 10.

Viadero, D. (2008, January 30). Teachers advised to 'get real' on race. *Education Week, 27*(21), 1,14.

Von Blum, P. (2008, September 3). Are advanced placement courses diminishing liberal arts education? *Education Week, 28*(2), 26–27.

Washor, E., & Mojkowski, C. (2006–07, December–January). What do you mean by rigor? *Educational Leadership, 64*(4), 84–87.

Wereschagin, M. (2007, September 11). Pittsburgh study: Teachers key in affecting pupils' success. *Pittsburgh Tribune-Review.* Retrieved February 9, 2009, from http://www.pittsburghlive.com/x/pittsburghtrib/news/cityregion/s_526792.html

Westerberg, T. (2007). *Creating the high schools of our choice.* Larchmont, NY: Eye on Education.

Whitman, D. (2008, Fall). An appeal to authority. *Education Next, 8*(4). Retrieved February 9, 2009, from http://www.hoover.org/publications/ednext/26967964.html

Wiggins, G. (2006, April/May). Healthier testing made easy: The idea of authentic assessment. *Edutopia Magazine.* Retrieved February 9, 2009, from http://www.edutopia.org/healthier-testing-made-easy

Wiggins, G., & McTighe, J. (1998). *Understanding by design.* Alexandria, VA: ASCD.

Wiggins, G., & McTighe, J. (2006, March). Examining the teaching life. *Educational Leadership, 63*(6), 26–29.

Wiggins, G., & McTighe, J. (2007). *Schooling by design.* Alexandria, VA: ASCD.

Wise, B. (2008, May). High schools at the tipping point. *Educational Leadership, 65*(8), 8–13.

Wurtzel, J. (2006). *Transforming high school teaching and learning: A district-wide design*. Washington, DC: The Aspen Institute.

Wurtzel, J. (2007, February). Getting at the core: New strategies for transforming HS teaching and learning. *Newsleader, 54*(6), 3, 10.

INDEX

Note: Page numbers followed by *f* indicate a figure.

About the Author

Dr. Tim R. Westerberg served as a high school principal for 26 years, the last 20 of which were at Littleton High School in Littleton, Colorado (1985–2005). Prior to entering school administration, Dr. Westerberg taught social studies and coached at the high school level in Illinois and Iowa. He earned his B.S. and M.A. degrees from the University of Iowa and his Ph.D. in Educational Administration from Iowa State University. He now resides in Dillon, Colorado.

In addition to his work as a teacher and administrator, Dr. Westerberg has been active in a variety of school transformation, staff development, and leadership training initiatives in Colorado, across the nation, and internationally. He served on the NASSP/Carnegie Foundation Commission on the Restructuring of the American High School, which produced the seminal report, *Breaking Ranks: Changing an American Institution*. He also played a significant role in the development of *Breaking Ranks II* which was released in February of 2004. His other recent professional activities include serving as a member of Robert Marzano's *What Works in Schools* professional development faculty, president of the Colorado Association of School Executives, member of the Colorado Commission for High School Improvement, and interim executive director of the Alliance for Quality Teaching.

Dr. Westerberg has received numerous awards in recognition of his service to the education profession, including being named as one of four finalists for the NASSP/Met Life Principal of the Year program in 1994, the Honor Administrator Award by the Colorado Music Educators Association in 1998, and the Department Service Award by the Colorado Association of Secondary School Principals in 1999. He currently serves as the president of the Alliance for Quality Teaching and is also author of the book, *Creating the High Schools of Our Choice* (2007), a principal's perspective on the realities of high school reform.

Related ASCD Resources: Becoming a Great High School

At the time of publication, the following ASCD resources were available; for the most up-to-date information about ASCD resources, go to www.ascd.org. ASCD stock numbers are noted in parentheses.

Print Products

Classroom Instruction That Works: Research-Based Strategies for Increasing Student Achievement by Robert J. Marzano, Debra J. Pickering, and Jane E. Pollock (#101010)

Doc: The Story of Dennis Littky and His Fight for a Better School by Susan Kammeraad-Campbell (#105056)

Educational Leadership, April 2007, The Prepared Graduates (#107032)

Educational Leadership, May 2008, Reshaping High Schools (#108027)

Education Update, October 2006, High School Reform in Philly 106023

Personalizing the High School Experience for Each Student by Joseph Dimartino and John H. Clarke (#107054)

Video

High Schools at Work: Creating Student-Centered Learning (one DVD with a comprehensive facilitator's guide) (#606117)

High Schools at Work: Engaging Students in Learning (one 30-minute videotape with Facilitator's Guide) (#406118)

High Schools at Work: Personalizing the School (one 30-minute videotape with Facilitator's Guide) (#406119)

THE WHOLE CHILD The Whole Child Initiative helps schools and communities create learning environments that allow students to be healthy, safe, engaged, supported, and challenged. To learn more about other books and resources that relate to the whole child, visit www.wholechildeducation.org.

For additional resources, visit us on the World Wide Web (http://www.ascd.org), send an e-mail message to member@ascd.org, call the ASCD Service Center (1-800-933-ASCD or 703-578-9600, then press 2), send a fax to 703-575-5400, or write to Information Services, ASCD, 1703 N. Beauregard St., Alexandria, VA 22311-1714 USA.